ANNE ODEKE

Anne is a writer, actor, and qualified secondary school drama teacher.

Her other plays have been performed at Queen's Theatre Hornchurch (*A Place for Me?*); Storyhouse Chester (*Little Women*) and the Bush Theatre (a one-woman version of *Princess Essex*), with commissions from HighTide (*Teaching and Booze Don't Mix*, and *Please Don't Let Him Be Black*) and BBC Radio 4 (*United Kingdoms*). She is also part of the Orange Tree Theatre's Writers Collective.

Other Titles in this Series

Annie Baker
THE ANTIPODES
THE FLICK
INFINITE LIFE
JOHN

Jez Butterworth
THE FERRYMAN
THE HILLS OF CALIFORNIA
JERUSALEM
JEZ BUTTERWORTH PLAYS: ONE
JEZ BUTTERWORTH PLAYS: TWO
MOJO
THE NIGHT HERON
PARLOUR SONG
THE RIVER
THE WINTERLING

Anupama Chandrasekhar
DISCONNECT
THE FATHER AND THE ASSASSIN
FREE OUTGOING
WHEN THE CROWS VISIT

Tearrance Arvelle Chisholm
BR'ER COTTON

Caryl Churchill
BLUE HEART
CHURCHILL PLAYS: THREE
CHURCHILL PLAYS: FOUR
CHURCHILL PLAYS: FIVE
CHURCHILL: SHORTS
CLOUD NINE
DING DONG THE WICKED
A DREAM PLAY after Strindberg
DRUNK ENOUGH TO SAY I LOVE YOU?
ESCAPED ALONE
FAR AWAY
GLASS. KILL. BLUEBEARD'S FRIENDS. IMP.
HERE WE GO
HOTEL
ICECREAM
LIGHT SHINING IN BUCKINGHAMSHIRE
LOVE AND INFORMATION
MAD FOREST
A NUMBER
PIGS AND DOGS
SEVEN JEWISH CHILDREN
THE SKRIKER
THIS IS A CHAIR
THYESTES after Seneca
TRAPS
WHAT IF IF ONLY

Natasha Gordon
NINE NIGHT

Dave Harris
TAMBO & BONES

Jeremy O. Harris
'DADDY': A MELODRAMA
SLAVE PLAY

Branden Jacobs-Jenkins
APPROPRIATE
THE COMEUPPANCE
GLORIA
AN OCTOROON

Arinzé Kene
GOD'S PROPERTY
GOOD DOG
LITTLE BABY JESUS & ESTATE WALLS
MISTY

Tony Kushner
ANGELS IN AMERICA –
  PARTS ONE AND TWO
CAROLINE, OR CHANGE
HOMEBODY/KABUL
THE VISIT, OR THE OLD LADY COMES TO
  CALL after Friedrich Dürrenmatt

Kimber Lee
UNTITLED F*CK M*SS S**GON PLAY

Tracy Letts
AUGUST: OSAGE COUNTY
KILLER JOE

Benedict Lombe
LAVA

Bruce Norris
CLYBOURNE PARK
DOWNSTATE
THE LOW ROAD
THE PAIN AND THE ITCH
PURPLE HEART

Lynn Nottage
CLYDE'S
CRUMBS FROM THE TABLE OF JOY
INTIMATE APPAREL
MLIMA'S TALE
RUINED
SWEAT

Gbolahan Obisesan
THE FISHERMEN after Chigozie Obioma
MAD ABOUT THE BOY

Chinonyerem Odimba
AMONGST THE REEDS
BLACK LOVE
PRINCESS & THE HUSTLER
UNKNOWN RIVERS

Suzan-Lori Parks
FATHER COMES HOME FROM THE
  WARS (PARTS 1, 2 & 3)
RED LETTER PLAYS
TOPDOG/UNDERDOG
WHITE NOISE

Winsome Pinnock
LEAVE TAKING
ROCKETS AND BLUE LIGHTS
TAKEN
TITUBA

debbie tucker green
BORN BAD
DEBBIE TUCKER GREEN PLAYS: ONE
DIRTY BUTTERFLY
EAR FOR EYE
HANG
NUT
A PROFOUNDLY AFFECTIONATE,
  PASSIONATE DEVOTION TO
  SOMEONE (– NOUN)
RANDOM
STONING MARY
TRADE & GENERATIONS
TRUTH AND RECONCILIATION

Tyrell Williams
RED PITCH

Danny Lee Wynter
BLACK SUPERHERO

Anne Odeke

PRINCESS ESSEX

NICK HERN BOOKS

London
www.nickhernbooks.co.uk

A Nick Hern Book

Princess Essex first published in Great Britain as a paperback original in 2024 by Nick Hern Books Limited, The Glasshouse, 49a Goldhawk Road, London, W12 8QP

Princess Essex copyright © 2024 Anne Odeke

Anne Odeke has asserted her right to be identified as the author of this work

Cover photography by The Other Richard; art direction by Kim Garrity

Designed and typeset by Nick Hern Books, London
Printed in Great Britain by Mimeo Ltd, Huntingdon, Cambridgeshire PE29 6XX

A CIP catalogue record for this book is available from the British Library

ISBN 978 1 83904 385 7

CAUTION All rights whatsoever in this play are strictly reserved. Requests to reproduce the text in whole or in part should be addressed to the publisher.

Amateur Performing Rights Applications for performance, including readings and excerpts, by amateurs in the English language should be addressed to the Performing Rights Manager, Nick Hern Books, The Glasshouse, 49a Goldhawk Road, London W12 8QP, *tel* +44 (0)20 8749 4953, *email* rights@nickhernbooks.co.uk, except as follows:

Australia: ORiGiN Theatrical, *tel* +61 (2) 8514 5201, *email* enquiries@originmusic.com.au, *web* www.origintheatrical.com.au

New Zealand: Play Bureau, 20 Rua Street, Mangapapa, Gisborne 4010, *tel* +64 21 258 3998, *email* info@playbureau.com

Professional Performing Rights Applications for performance by professionals in any medium and in any language throughout the world (and by amateurs in the United States of America and Canada) should be addressed to The Haworth Agency, Studio 103, Babel Studios, 158b Kentish Town Road, London, NW5 2AG, *tel* +44 (0)20 4551 2607, *email* permissions@haworthagency.co.uk

No performance of any kind may be given unless a licence has been obtained. Applications should be made before rehearsals begin. Publication of this play does not necessarily indicate its availability for amateur performance.

www.nickhernbooks.co.uk/environmental-policy

Princess Essex was first performed at Shakespeare's Globe, London, on 19 September 2024 (previews from 13 September). The cast was as follows:

MR BACON/ENSEMBLE	Matthew Ashforde
COLONEL HARRIS/MR ROMFORD RECORDER/ENSEMBLE/COVER	Nigel Barrett
EVE/ENSEMBLE	Janai Bartlett/ Kyla Semper
EDWARD VII/COUSIN ARTHUR/ COUNCILLOR PERRY (FOLKESTONE)/VICAR/ ENSEMBLE	John Cummins
BATWA/COUNCILLOR REGINALD (SOUTHEND)/ ENSEMBLE	Alison Halstead
MRS BUGLE/COUNCILLOR CECIL (SOUTHEND)/ENSEMBLE	Lizzie Hopley
MAYOR PEPPER (FOLKESTONE)/ COUNCILLOR BERNARD (SOUTHEND)/DEBT COLLECTOR 2/ JOANNA'S DAD/MR HORNCHURCH HERALD/ENSEMBLE	Tyreke Leslie
NUN/MR SOUTHEND STANDARD/ ENSEMBLE/COVER	Sophie Mercell
COUNCILLOR BERTIE (FOLKESTONE)/ MR DAGENHAM DAILY/DEBT COLLECTOR 1/COUNCILLOR GEOFFREY (SOUTHEND)/COURTIER/ ELISE (MISS BELGIUM)/ENSEMBLE	Syakira Moeladi
MRS BACON/PEACHES (MISS USA)/ COUNCILLOR RALPH (SOUTHEND)/ ENSEMBLE	Jamie-Rose Monk
JOANNA/PRINCESS DINUBOLU	Anne Odeke
VIOLET/JOANNA'S MUM/ COUNCILLOR CLIVE (SOUTHEND)/ ENSEMBLE	Eloise Secker

MAYOR INGRAM/COUNCILLOR THOMAS (FOLKESTONE)/ ENSEMBLE	Simon Startin
HARRIET/COUNCILLOR ROBERT (SOUTHEND)/ENSEMBLE	Yasmin Taheri

MUSICIANS

Banjo/Guitar	Ashley Blasse
Percussion	Louise Duggan
Saxophone/Clarinet	Melanie Henry
Bass Trombone/Tuba	Yusuf Narcin
Casting Director	Becky Paris CDG
Composer	Simon Slater
Costume Supervisor	Isobel Pellow
Designer	Hayley Grindle
Director	Robin Belfield
Dramaturg	Sarah Dickenson
Fight Director	Bethan Clark
Globe Associate – Movement	Glynn MacDonald
Head of Voice	Tess Dignan
Movement and Intimacy Director	Ingrid Mackinnon
Resident Assistant Director	Priya Patel Appleby
Voice and Accent Coach	Ellen Hartley
Wellbeing, Cultural and Diversity Consultant	Carol Cumberbatch

With thanks to: Margaret Borton, Elise Ellis, Lucy Farrant, Wayne Glover-Stuart, Nic Wass, Rachel Yvonne, and The Globe's 2024 summer season volunteer stewards.

The Essex Princess, a monologue, was commissioned for *Misfits* by Queen's Theatre Hornchurch and first performed on 12 November 2020. This evolved into a first version of *Princess Essex*, a one-person play that toured with the support of Arts Council England, Queen's Theatre Hornchurch, Matthew Schmolle, The Mercury Theatre Colchester, Creative Estuary and the South Essex African & Caribbean Association (SEACA) from February 2022.

Shakespeare's Globe: Best Friends of *Princess Essex*
Catherine Arnfield, Jennifer Barton, Alice, Penny Calder, Doug Connor, Hema Coombes, Derrick Dale, Peter Davio, Ann Dunbar, Anne Dunlop, Thomas Eugster, Janis Fawn, Valerie Fletcher, Krisztina Földi & Alan Short, Lord Hannan, Chris Hennock, Elizabeth Hodgkiss, Rebecca Hume, Kate & Barry Jones, Sierra McLeod, Peter Nathanielsz, Professor Arthur Petersen, Samuel Pickard, Robin Roads, Mr & Mrs Roller, Anne Rowley, Raymond Rulach, D Ryan, Eileen & Michael Sanderson, Paul Shantic and Shell Mercurio, Anne Smith, Michael Smith, Davis Taggart, Philip Teale, Margaret Thomas, Lara Waterfield, Edwin Williams, Sarah Wilton, Martin Wink, Jess Withington

Characters
in order of appearance

The BAND
JOANNA/PRINCESS DINUBOLU
PUNCH AND JUDY ENTERTAINER (BAXTER)
FISHERMAN (AMOS)
MRS LONDON (PEGGY)
MR LONDON (HAROLD)
IRRATIONALLY ANGRY WOMAN (PATIENCE)
TICKETER (JOSEPHINE)
MRS BUGLE (STELLA)
MAYOR PEPPER (ALBERT)
TOWN COUNCILLOR PERRY (*Folkestone*)
TOWN COUNCILLOR THOMAS (*Folkestone*)
TOWN COUNCILLOR BERTIE (*Folkestone*)
PEACHES, *American beauty pageant contestant*
MR BACON (PARSLEY)
MR SOUTHEND STANDARD (ALFIE)
MR ROMFORD RECORDER (HECTOR)
MR DAGENHAM DAILY (FRED)
MAYOR INGRAM (JAMES)

VIOLET MAY INGRAM
TOWN COUNCILLOR BERNARD (*Southend-on-Sea*)
COLONEL HARRIS (JAMES)
THE GREAT BATWA
VICAR (REVERAND JACOB CRISPIN)
MEMBERS OF THE CONGREGATION
DEBT COLLECTOR 1 (HORACE)
DEBT COLLECTOR 2 (DICK)
TWO GIRLS (EILEEN *and* BESSIE)
BOBBY (BLODWEN)
CHIMNEY SWEEP (JOHN)
BISCUIT LADY (SOPHIE)

CHARACTERS

NURSE (LESLEY)
STRONG MAN (CLEMENT)
SCHOOLTEACHER (WALTER)
MOTHER WITH BABY IN PRAM (MAUDE)
COUSIN ARTHUR, *a postman*
MRS BACON (JESSIE)
HARRIET
JOANNA'S MUM (JOANNA)
JOANNA'S MUM'S FRIEND (CHRISTINE)
JOANNA'S DAD (MICHAEL)
SUITED BAND MEMBER (GILBERT)
NUN (SISTER MARIA)
WOMAN NOT INTERESTED IN BEAUTY PAGEANTS 1 (CLEMENTINE)
WOMAN NOT INTERESTED IN BEAUTY PAGEANTS 2 (DAISY)
LILIAN EDWARDS
MIRIAM CARTER

LENA SABINE KOPPENSTEINER, *Austria*
CATALINA MARGARITA HERNANDEZ, *Spain*
MARTINA FRANCESCA GUILIA ISABELLA AGOSTINELLI, *Italy*
TOWN COUNCILLOR ROBERT (*Southend-on-Sea*)
TOWN COUNCILLOR CLIVE (*Southend-on-Sea*)
TOWN COUNCILLOR GEOFFREY (*Southend-on-Sea*)
TOWN COUNCILLOR RALPH (*Southend-on-Sea*)
TOWN COUNCILLOR CECIL (*Southend-on-Sea*)
TOWN COUNCILLOR REGINALD (*Southend-on-Sea*)
KING EDWARD VII
COURTIER (FRANZ)
COURTIERS
MUSICIAN
EVE
ELISE, *beauty pageant contestant – Belgium*
SNEZANA, *beauty pageant contestant – Serbia*
INGEBORG, *beauty pageant contestant – Norway*
FRIEDA, *beauty pageant contestant – Germany*

Notes on Text

A forward slash (/) denotes overlapping dialogue.

A dash (–) denotes an interruption or unfinished thought.

Text in **bold** is sung.

This text went to press before the end of rehearsals and so may differ slightly from the play as performed.

ACT ONE

Scene One

Enter the BAND *onto Juliet's balcony. Suited, they make their way to their instruments, and sit. They begin to play music that is magical, soft, gentle.*

Enter a distracted JOANNA *through the centre-stage doors, dressed in her maid attire.*

We are in Southend-on-Sea – specifically we are in JOANNA*'s daydream.* JOANNA *is in the attic of the Bugle residence – two weeks before the big event.*

As she creeps in, enter the ENSEMBLE *grouped together. They are, at this moment, an echo of* JOANNA*'s thoughts. They watch her curiously.*

After a short time, JOANNA *senses the* ENSEMBLE *are watching her and so slowly turns around. As her eyes meet theirs, they smile at her and wave.*

What ensues is a playful game between the two, similar to that of Grandma's Footsteps; JOANNA *teases the* ENSEMBLE *two more times, by running away, stopping and suddenly turning around to greet them – each time the movements of all involved grow bigger and bigger.*

JOANNA *then finds herself looking out across the audience. She closes her eyes and hums the starting notes of 'I Do Like to Be Beside the Seaside'. The* ENSEMBLE *echo her singing, and before we know it the* BAND, ENSEMBLE *and* JOANNA *are all singing the song.* JOANNA *and the* ENSEMBLE *also dance in a way that is inspired by a cockney knees-up. It suggests the people of the Southend-on-Sea are happy, upbeat, bright-eyed and optimistic – perhaps too good to be true?*

ENSEMBLE.
> Oh! I do like to be beside the seaside!
> I do like to be beside the sea!
> Oh I do like to stroll along the prom, prom, prom!
> Where the brass bands play, 'Tiddely-om-pom-pom!'
>
> So just let me be beside the seaside!
> I'll be beside myself with glee –
> And there's lots of girls beside
> I should like to be beside, beside the seaside
> Beside the sea!

We are in Southend-on-Sea – specifically we are in Joanna's daydream. JOANNA is in the attic of the Bugle residence – two weeks before the Miss Southend 1908 beauty pageant.

Enter JOANNA through the centre-stage doors, dressed in her maid attire.

JOANNA *breathes in the estuary air.*

JOANNA (*addressing the audience*). Ahh, Southend-on-Sea!

The ENSEMBLE then morph into a kaleidoscope of characters one might find in Southend-on-Sea in 1908, including a PUNCH AND JUDY ENTERTAINER, FISHERMAN, etc. The mood is one of great joy.

PUNCH AND JUDY ENTERTAINER (*cheerfully*). Morning Joanna!

JOANNA. There ain't no greater place in the entire world, coz 'ere you see, we have it all: the beach, the cliffs, a statue of Queen Victoria –

FISHERMAN (*cheerfully*). Morning Joanna!

JOANNA. – the world's longest pier, *sea*gulls, the *sea*front, the *sea*side – which is nuffing less than ironic because as every local will tell ya –

The ENSEMBLE stop and face the audience.

ALL (*in a manner that implies 'Actually…'*). *That* ain't a sea at all, *that* is an estuary, *that* is the River Thames.

ACT ONE, SCENE ONE   13

The ENSEMBLE *return to their sequence. Enter* MR LONDON *and* MRS LONDON *dressed in bathing suits and weighed down by several deckchairs, an umbrella, a windbreaker, a picnic basket, and a large cuddly toy one can only assume they won at the Kursaal.*

JOANNA. So it's mad to fink, yeah, that Londoners, *fousands* of 'em, each year, *they* flock to *us* – (*Spots* MR *and* MRS LONDON.) and well, yer can always tell a London-a because –

(*Turning to* MRS LONDON *and* MR LONDON.) Morning!

MR LONDON *and* MRS LONDON *growl and snarl at* JOANNA. JOANNA *can't make out what they are saying.*

Across the water and staring back at us, sits a county so dull, so void of any excitement, that no Southender dare ever swim across to it for fear of neva coming back – a county so boring that the only title they could come up for it was '*Garden of England*', and that place, is Kent.

IRRATIONALLY ANGRY WOMAN. Burn in 'ell, Kent! I 'ate ya!

JOANNA. This rivalry between us, yeah, is only seven years young, and it all started in 1901, son, because they woz jealous of us. (*Eyes begin to light up.*) They are jealous of the fact that 'ere, in Southend-on-Sea, we 'av what is (and undeniably) the largest and greatest entertainment building in the whole of Europe, a building so big, so beautiful, it puts the Taj Mahal to shame, and that building is… (*Spins around the face the Kursaal.*) the Kursaal!!!

A beat as the ENSEMBLE *are hit by the mere mentioning of the Kursaal. They experience a euphoria, and so now begin to move as though they are floating in air.*

MRS BUGLE (*from under the stage*). Joanna! – Joanna!

Hearing MRS BUGLE, *the* ENSEMBLE *quickly disperse.*

JOANNA. The Kursaal, meaning 'cure hall', is a place where entertainment can cure you all of your woes. Behind its doors lies everyfing you could ever dream of: a circus ring, concert 'all, dining 'all, a billiard saloon, shops; nigh on forty of 'em – a menagerie – complete with lions, tigers and polar bears –

MRS BUGLE (*from under the stage*). Joanna! – Joanna!

JOANNA. – a football pitch, athletics ground, a trotting track, hoopla stands, a hippodrome, and that's just to name a few.

For Southenders, the Kursaal, it's *in* us – perhaps somehow even, it *is* us? It's 'ard to remember nah what life woz like wivaat it –

The trapdoor slams open.

MRS BUGLE (*from under the stage*). Joanna!

We see a long ladder gradually emerging from the trap.

JOANNA. – and at centre of it all, lies a ballroom with a stage that ain't just the envy of Essex, of England even, but of the entire Empire!

We see MRS BUGLE's head pop out from the pit. She speaks to JOANNA.

MRS BUGLE. Joanna! Joanna!!

JOANNA *snaps out of her daydream*. MRS BUGLE – *a middle-class, Southend socialite – emerges from the trap. She remains speaking to* JOANNA *whilst still holding on to the ladder.*

Joanna! What are you doing up here in the attic? (*Looking around.*) Are you talking to yourself?

MRS BUGLE *gestures for* JOANNA *to help her off the ladder.* JOANNA *does so.*

JOANNA. Nuffin, Mrs Bugle, I was just –

MRS BUGLE. Were you hiding?

JOANNA (*obviously 'yes'*). No.

MRS BUGLE (*patronisingly, knowing she's caught her out*). I think you were, Joanna. Anyone would think you don't enjoy dusting / the –

ACT ONE, SCENE ONE   15

JOANNA. / I didn't / say –

MRS BUGLE (*patronising*). / Look, I get it. Really I do. Life's hard. I know. It's hard for us all. (*Confessing*.) Sometimes, I can't keep up with the latest Parisian trends, or what cake one should now bring to a bake sale. But we mustn't let our feelings show, and well… if that means one needs to creep up into the attic for a little cry now and again, one likes to think that their employer would understand.

JOANNA. That's very kind of you Mrs Bugle / but –

MRS BUGLE. / Have you heard the latest gossip from Folkestone?

JOANNA (*surprised*). Er, 'Folkestone'?? Er, sorry, Folkestone? Er… er, no I ain't – what they done, nah?

MRS BUGLE. Heavens, just when you think those Kentish cretins couldn't stoop any lower, is there really nothing they won't try?

JOANNA. Why, wot they done?

MRS BUGLE. They're planning on holding an event, and a *ridiculous* one at that.

JOANNA (*concerned*). Like, wot?

MRS BUGLE. I'll tell you like what – they're planning on holding / a beauty pageant –

Enter MAYOR PEPPER *in his civic regalia, being quickly followed by* TOWN COUNCILLORS PERRY, THOMAS *and* BERTIE. *We are at a Town Council meeting in Folkestone.*

MAYOR PEPPER. '*A beauty pageant.*'

PERRY (*confused*). A what?

MAYOR PEPPER. '*A beauty pageant.*'

THOMAS. What in God's name, Pepper, is –

MAYOR PEPPER. Was chatting about it to an American chum of mine. Apparently they're all the rage over there. Women put on their best frocks, do their hair, that sort of thing, and then the best looking gal gets... (*Removes a tiara from his jacket pocket.*) a crown.

THOMAS (*mockingly*). '*A crown*'?!

THOMAS, PERRY *and* BERTIE *laugh. It's a stupid idea. From his pocket,* MAYOR PEPPER *hands* JOANNA *a tiara.* JOANNA *takes it and stares at it.*

MAYOR PEPPER (*earnestly*). Laugh all you like, gentlemen, but seven years ago Kent missed a trick with the Kursaal – I wonder if we're willing to make the same mistake again?

Gulp. ALL *ponder.*

PERRY. And the girls – they'd just come to us – would they??

BERTIE (*enquiring*). From all over Britain??

MAYOR PEPPER (*a brilliant thought comes to him*). Why not make it international, since everyone's gone bonkers with Britain this year hosting the Olympics, that – (*Exaggerated French accent.*) Entente Cordial, His Majesty's exhibit, and that there African village – it only makes sense.

THOMAS (*smirking*). I don't see why not.

BERTIE (*yearning*). Anything to get us out of Southend's shadow.

PERRY. So, one of these *international thingies*, that would make Folkestone, the first town in the whole of England to do so? – Ever?

MAYOR PEPPER (*smugly*). I believe so, Perry, yes.

ALL *look to one another, before nodding agreeingly.*

BERTIE (*smirking*). I think a '*beauty pageant*', sounds delightful!!

As the COUNCILLORS *all shake hands and congratulate one another, enter* PEACHES *through the stage-right door. No one sees her except* JOANNA. *She wears a sash that reads 'Miss Tennessee 1908'. She makes her way across the stage, and exits through the yard. As she passes* JOANNA, *she takes the tiara and places it on her own head.* JOANNA *watches her go.*

PERRY (*excitedly*). Shall I contact the papers, Mayor Pepper?

MAYOR PEPPER. Yes, do!

PERRY (*giddy*). Goodness! Folkestone to hold – (*Painting the headline with his hands.*) 'Britain's First Ever International Beauty Pageant'.

THOMAS (*looking out to the audience, as though he's looking across the estuary*). My God, those cockle-eating, cockney wannabes won't know what's hit them!

MAYOR PEPPER, PERRY *and* BERTIE *jeer.*

THOMAS. Nothing but a bunch of sex-obsessed –

BERTIE. – especially the females (!) –

THOMAS. – lazy-spoken imbeciles!

PERRY. I ask you, how hard is it to pronounce a 't'?!

BERTIE. I say we get our best men, line 'em up along the estuary and just fire!

MAYOR PEPPER, THOMAS, PERRY *and* BERTIE. Hear, hear!

A blast of 'English Country Garden' as MAYOR PEPPER, THOMAS, PERRY *and* BERTIE *exit. As soon as the doors slam shut* (*in time with the last chord of the song*), MRS BUGLE *says* –

MRS BUGLE (*annoyed*). Joanna?! *Joanna?!*

JOANNA. D'ya reckon I could enta?

MRS BUGLE (*screwing her nose up*). Oh Joanna, aren't you jolly? Now, come here.

JOANNA *does as she is told.*

Close your eyes! Palms out! And ask yourself, what you do you love most in the world?

A giddy MRS BUGLE *places two tickets with red bow on top into* JOANNA*'s hands.*

JOANNA (*smiling*). Chocolate.

MRS BUGLE (*a tad disappointed, but still excited*). Anything else?

JOANNA. Well obviously I love / the Kursaal –

MRS BUGLE (*unable to contain her excitement*). THE KURSAAL! – SO HOW ABOUT TWO FRONT-ROW TICKETS FOR TONIGHT'S SHOW, TO SEE *'THE GREAT BATWA'*?!!!

JOANNA *opens her eyes and sees the tickets. She can't believe it.*

JOANNA (*happy but confused*). Is this a joke, Mrs Bugle… are you playing me around or wot??

MRS BUGLE. Of course not! Mr Bugle's out with the boys again tonight, so I wondered if you might like to escort me?

JOANNA (*trying to contain her joy*). Ta *the Kursaal*??

MRS BUGLE. Yes!

JOANNA (*touched by Mrs Bugle's kindness*). Well, of course. I'd love ta.

MRS BUGLE (*smiling*). Good! Then in that case, I'll need you to dress me. Anyone who's anyone will be there tonight, so chins up and let's put on our best hats!

Exit an excited MRS BUGLE *and* JOANNA. JOANNA *gives a nod to the audience as she leaves.*

Scene Two

It's now evening. Same day.

The stage transforms into the Kursaal. As the doors open, a piece of red carpet is rolled across the stage – upstage-centre to downstage-centre.

ACT ONE, SCENE TWO 19

Enter MR BACON, MR SOUTHEND STANDARD, MR ROMFORD RECORDER *and* MR DAGENHAM DAILY, *who has a large camera on a tripod. The journalists all set themselves up ready for the VIP guests' arrival.*

Enter also TICKETER, *who puts up posters on the pillars advertising tonight's show, 'Colonel Harris presents the Great Batwa! FINAL CHANCE! LAST FEW TICKETS!' Once set, they then stand upstage by the double doors in order to greet guests as they enter.*

Enter then MAYOR INGRAM, VIOLET *and* TOWN COUNCILLOR BERNARD *from the yard.*

Both VIOLET *and* MAYOR INGRAM *stand on the red carpet* – COUNCILLOR BERNARD *stands away from it but near* MAYOR INGRAM.

MR BACON *greets* MAYOR INGRAM. *The two pose, shaking hands for the camera.*

MR DAGENHAM DAILY. Just a little longa, gentlemen. (*Banter.*) Any chance you could act like you like one another?

MR BACON, MAYOR INGRAM, BERNARD, MR SOUTHEND STANDARD *and* MR ROMFORD RECORDER *laugh.*

MAYOR INGRAM (*banter*). Is it that obvious, Fred?

MR BACON, MAYOR INGRAM *and* BERNARD *laugh smugly again.* MR BACON *and* MAYOR INGRAM *remain holding hands – Edwardian photos took a while.*

MR SOUTHEND STANDARD (*interjecting*). *Mr Mayor! Mayor Ingram! Southend Standard*! You looking forward to the show tonight?

MAYOR INGRAM (*ever the professional*). Of course I am, I've only heard *great* things about 'The Great Batwa'.

MR SOUTHEND STANDARD. And what are you expecting from tonight?

MAYOR INGRAM (*with a smirk*). Well anyone who comes to the Kursaal expects to be entertained, so entertainment I guess.

MR DAGENHAM DAILY (*implying they can let go*). Thank you, gentlemen, you can let go nah.

VIOLET *steps forward, and cuddles* MAYOR INGRAM*'s arm. She's very aware of the camera.*

MR ROMFORD RECORDER. *Mr Bacon! – Romford Recorder* – you excited about the show?

MR BACON (*surprised to even be asked*). Me?! Yeah. Yeah, I am.

MR ROMFORD RECORDER. Why??

MR BACON. Well, as manager I can tell ya, we ain't 'ad nuffink quite like this at the Kursaal / before.

MAYOR INGRAM. / Having a show such as this, brings the Kursaal another step closer to becoming the largest entertainment complex –

MAYOR INGRAM *and* MR BACON (*almost in sync but not quite*). – not only in Europe, but the entire world.

MR DAGENHAM DAILY. *Mr Mayor – Dagenham Daily –* any words for the people of Folkestone?

MAYOR INGRAM (*dismissively*). No.

MR DAGENHAM DAILY. Come nah, Mr Mayor. You must 'av sunink to say about the upcoming international pageant? Rumour has it, it's gonna knock Southend off the top spot.

MAYOR INGRAM (*with a slight hesitation*). I doubt that very much. Tell them, '*Southend wishes them the very best of luck with it all.*' (*Smirking.*) Certainly sounds like they'll need it.

BERNARD *laughs*.

MR SOUTHEND STANDARD. *Miss Ingram!* You finking of entering?

VIOLET. Well funnily enough, I have always wanted to –

ACT ONE, SCENE TWO   21

MAYOR INGRAM. I'm afraid Violet's a very busy girl, and hasn't the time. Besides, it wouldn't be fair on the others, she'd win by a mile.

MR DAGENHAM DAILY (*interjecting*). What a shame. 'Ere, Miss Ingram!? Mr Mayor!? Can we get a picture? Father and daughter like.

MAYOR INGRAM. Course.

MAYOR INGRAM *puts his arm around a clearly very affronted* VIOLET.

MR BACON. I think that's quite enough, gentlemen – the mayor's come out tonight to enjoy himself.

MAYOR INGRAM (*under his breath*). I can speak for myself, Bacon.

MR BACON. Of course, sir, I wasn't –

VIOLET *storms off ahead and upstage through the double doors.* MAYOR INGRAM *signals to* BERNARD *to follow her.*

MAYOR INGRAM (*taking control of the situation*). Er, would you excuse us, gentlemen? It's quite time we all found our seats.

Exit MAYOR INGRAM.

Enter an excited MRS BUGLE *with* JOANNA *in tow from the yard.* MRS BUGLE *wears an extremely large, ornate hat – we feel for anyone who has to sit behind her. By comparison,* JOANNA*'s hat is very, very simple.*

As MRS BUGLE *steps onto the red carpet, so too does* JOANNA*, just behind her.* MRS BUGLE *is greeted by* MR BACON.

MRS BUGLE. Good evening, Mr Bacon!

MR BACON (*greeting her*). *Mrs Bugle!* – no Mr Bugle?

MRS BUGLE. No. I thought this evening it might be best to bring my, erm...

MR SOUTHEND STANDARD. *Mrs Bugle!* Beautiful hat for a socialite like yourself. French?

MRS BUGLE (*proudly*). Oui…!

MR ROMFORD RECORDER. *Mrs Bugle!* You finking of entering the Folkestone pageant??

MRS BUGLE (*surprised*). Me?? (*Snorts.*) I'm a happily married woman. I wouldn't dream of it.

MR DAGENHAM DAILY. 'Ere, *Mrs Bugle*, *Mr Bacon*, can we get a fo-ta?

MRS BUGLE. Of course.

MRS BUGLE and MR BACON *pose.* MR DAGENHAM DAILY *goes to take the photo, but through the lens spots* JOANNA.

MR DAGENHAM DAILY (*annoyed, to* JOANNA). 'Ere, luv, can you move? You're spoiling the picture.

JOANNA is wounded. As such, she apologetically and quickly jumps off of the red carpet.

Suddenly we hear the sound of African drumming.

Exit MR SOUTHEND STANDARD, MR ROMFORD RECORDER *and* MR DAGENHAM DAILY.

MR BACON, *politely encouraging* MRS BUGLE *to move along so the show can begin on time, gestures for her to walk in front of him and up through the centre-stage doors.*

MR BACON (*warmly*). Mrs Bugle? After you…

MRS BUGLE *excitedly exits upstage. She gestures for* JOANNA *to quickly follow her.* JOANNA *does so, but walks beside the red carpet. The two make their way up and onto Juliet's balcony to watch the show.*

As the women leave, MR BACON *quickly rolls up the red carpet and exits through the centre-stage doors. As he does,* TICKETER *shuts the centre-stage doors behind him.*

ACT ONE, SCENE TWO 23

Enter COLONEL HARRIS. *Dressed in traditional explorer/safari attire, he slowly makes his way down to the downstage-right corner and stops to address the audience.*

COLONEL HARRIS. I, am Colonel John Benjamin Harris.

A lifetime ago, so it seems, I was a man of God – still am in fact – but no longer a missionary, no, God, you see, invited me to take a rather different path – (*Gesturing to his attire.*) and though confused at the time as to why he might have done so, one knows better than to question the Almighty.

I remember the very first time I stepped into the Ituri Forest; the Congo. I knew that no words could ever paint so beautiful a picture of all that stood before me – trees as far and as tall as the eye could see; countless shades of emerald green; rich.

Then all of a sudden I heard the pounding of drums – the rhythm possessed me, and within moments I found myself staring face to face with... well –

For fear of my fellow countrymen doubting my every word, I chose to bring a little piece of that forest back with me. Would you like to see it?

SOUTHEND! Allow me to present to you, all the way from the Dark Continent, the one, the only, *the Great Batwa*!!!

The sound of a large gong being hit, followed by drumming – ALL the drumming! The centre doors slowly peel open and there, standing centre is THE GREAT BATWA. *He is dressed in a skimpy grass-like skirt, no shoes, with an armband and necklace made of white beads.*

There are several options as to how the actor may prefer to enter the stage: 1) They may wish to simply walk down and hit centre, just downstage of the pillars; 2) They may decide to carry out some form of 'tribal dance', again landing just downstage of the pillars; 3) They may cartwheel, backflip, forward roll until they are just downstage of the pillars.

Presenting, '*The pygmy*'!

From his pocket, COLONEL HARRIS *takes out a small piece of bread.* BATWA *runs over to him, takes it from him and devours it.*

Large lips; thick. Dark eyes. Wide nose. Features that are ordinarily very ugly, but this all makes sense when we learn that the Negro skull has many approximations to that of the ape.

COLONEL HARRIS *claps his hands –* BATWA *climbs up the stage-right pillar.* COLONEL HARRIS *continues addressing the audience.*

Notice the skin to be dull in colour yet velvet to the touch, and the hair: black, thick and curly, some might even go as far as to say 'beautiful', and yet the most striking peculiarity is that of the relative dimensions of the various parts of the body, most noticeably, that of the pygmy's height.

COLONEL HARRIS *claps his hands again: an instruction to* BATWA *to get down.* BATWA *does so.*

Indifferent to clothing, the pygmy prefers instead to dress – or should that be, not dress – in a fashion quite unlike his Europeans counterparts. When trying to ascertain why, I found myself met only with a series of gabblings, thus proving the pygmy to be incapable of any real speech.

On behalf of myself and Batwa I'd like to say *merci beaucoup to you*, Southend, for making us feel oh so very welcome – say goodbye, Batwa –

BATWA *waves to the audience, almost childlike.*

Goodnight, ladies and gentlemen, and may God bless each and every one you.

Together COLONEL HARRIS *and* BATWA *exit through the centre doors. Exit* MRS BUGLE *also.*

A shaken JOANNA *is left staring at the empty stage for a moment. She then turns and exits.*

Scene Three

It's the next day.

We are outside St Mary's Church, Southend-on-Sea. Enter a deeply troubled JOANNA. She addresses the audience.

JOANNA. Today's different. Today doesn't feel like yesterday, or last week, it feels... *different*. And by 'it' I fink I might mean, 'me'. Today I feel different; I feel outside of meself. Does that make sense? Like, some'ow, in seeing another, othered – another like me, othered, I some'ow, saw me for the very first time: '*large lips, dark eyes, wide nose; features that are ordinarily very ugly*'. But then one man's words do not speak for mankind??

Through the centre-stage doors enter VICAR and the CONGREGATION, amongst whom are MRS BUGLE (carrying a parasol) and JOANNA. The CONGREGATION shake the VICAR's hand and thank him as they leave.

MRS BUGLE (*shaking the VICAR's hand*). A wonderful service, Vicar, thank you.

VICAR (*smiling*). You're too kind, Mrs Bugle.

MRS BUGLE. Not at all.

MRS BUGLE and JOANNA go to walk downstage.

VICAR (*inquisitively*). Oh Mrs Bugle, no Mr Bugle again??

MRS BUGLE (*embarrassed*). I'm afraid he's indisposed (again).

VICAR. Of course. Do thank him for the terribly kind donation and much thanks to your good self.

MRS BUGLE smiles and tries her best to hide her shame. VICAR returns to shaking the hands of his parishioners.

MRS BUGLE tries her best to open her parasol but finds it to not be behaving itself.

MRS BUGLE (*annoyed*). Is there a problem, Joanna? You've been at odds all morning. It's driving me mad.

JOANNA *shrugs*.

(*Passive-aggressively*.) Well, whatever is it, could you please not burden our Lord with it, it is his day of rest.

JOANNA. I don't fink it's God I've a problem with.

MRS BUGLE. Then who? (*Feeling rather put out*.) Not *me*?!

JOANNA. –

MRS BUGLE. Well it can't be, not after such a pleasant evening together?

JOANNA. '*Pleasant*'? What was pleasant about seeing *the Great Batwa* have to dance for his dinner, be spoken about like he were a fing; like he weren't even there?

MRS BUGLE (*it sudden dawns on her*). Ohhh! Is that what this is about?? Your sense of kin.

JOANNA. –

MRS BUGLE. Coz you're not, you know. You're not like him. I mean obviously you are a – but you're not, a real one.

JOANNA (*insulted*). I beg your pardon?

MRS BUGLE (*distastefully*). Besides, you don't really look anything like *that*.

JOANNA. Like, *what*?

MRS BUGLE. I mean you do, but... (*Trying to find the words*.)

JOANNA (*bluntly*). What would yer say, if I said I wanted to go to Folkestone?

MRS BUGLE (*flippantly*). Well I'd say, 'If that's the punchline, what was the joke?'

JOANNA (*serious*). No joke. What if I said I wanted to enter the beauty pageant there?

MRS BUGLE. Oh Joanna. Please. I'm not in the jolliest of moods.

ACT ONE, SCENE THREE 27

JOANNA. I mean it. I'm just asking ya. What would you say?? (*Slightly raising her voice.*) Go on, wot'd yer say?!

MRS BUGLE (*aware of those around them*). Ssh! – I'd say... (*Trying the find the word but unable to.*) well, I don't really know.

JOANNA. D'ya fink I'd win? – D'ya fink someone like me, could win?

MRS BUGLE (*defeated*). Oh Joanna, this has all got terribly out of hand.

JOANNA. I'm just asking. You look at me face every day.

MRS BUGLE. Look, can we start again?

Beat.

I'm sorry you're upset because you believe the little man to be being treated badly.

JOANNA (*raising her voice in frustration*). He is!

With JOANNA *having raised her voice again,* MRS BUGLE *becomes even more aware of those around her.*

MRS BUGLE (*annoyed*). Is he, Joanna? Is he?! Because you tell me when else in his life he'd have had the chance to travel the world, *eat bread*?! Last week he found himself at Buckingham Palace, in front of the King, don't you know?

JOANNA (*affronted*). So what?

MRS BUGLE (*shocked*). Joanna, you forget yourself.

JOANNA. That colonel ought be ashamed of himself taking advantage of such an innocent soul!

MRS BUGLE. Well in that case, ought you not to be ashamed of yourself, for I didn't see you last night at any point walking out.

Beat.

JOANNA *is wounded by* MRS BUGLE's *words.*

Beat.

JOANNA *goes to leave.*

(*In a panic.*) Joanna! Joanna? Come back right this instant! Joanna! Joanna?! Where are you going? –

JOANNA (*calmly*). First, I'm gonna collect me fings, and then I'm gonna go and *save the Great Batwa*.

JOANNA *makes to exit through the stage-left door.*

MRS BUGLE (*shocked*). Oh Joanna, that's preposterous. (*Calling after her.*) Joanna! Joanna!

JOANNA *suddenly turns back around to* MRS BUGLE.

JOANNA. Goodbye, Mrs Bugle!

JOANNA *exits*.

MRS BUGLE. Joanna?! – Joanna?! If you go, we shan't have you back, I mean it. (*Worried.*) Joanna? Joanna?

A panicked MRS BUGLE *toddles after* JOANNA, *and exits.*

Scene Four

A rhythm plays. It puts the 'sex' in 'Essex' – it's geezery. We're back at the Kursaal. Enter TICKETER, *who puts up a sign saying 'Stage Door' above the door stage-right. The sign is a tad rundown, and a little rusty from the 'sea' air.*

Enter DEBT COLLECTOR 1 *and* DEBT COLLECTOR 2. *They knock on the stage door.* TICKETER *opens the door. We can't quite hear what's being said but it would appear that* DEBT COLLECTOR 1 *and* DEBT COLLECTOR 2 *are asking if* MR BACON *is 'available for a little chat'.*

Enter MR BACON *draped in an expensive fur coat, and being distracted by two* GIRLS *weighing on his arms. He gives off the air of an absolute don; Ian Dury swagger.* TICKETER *points to* MR BACON *and quickly shuts the door.* DEBT COLLECTOR

1 *and* DEBT COLLECTOR 2 *turn and glare at him.*

Spoken word / Song – 'The Big I Am'

MR BACON.
   Ladies! Please! Give us a bit of space

GIRLS.
   But we love you, Mr Bacon!

MR BACON.
   I'm aware dat's the case
   Nuffing to do with the Kursaal
   That I 'old the keys?

GIRLS.
   No of course it isn't, Parsley!

MR BACON.
   Don't calls us that please
   Look, it ain't that I ain't flattered
   Or that you ain't me type
   But I got me missus, yeah – ?

GIRLS.
   And?!

MR BACON (*speaking out of rhythm, to the audience*). And I'm telling ya, if she eva found aat that I'd even fought abaat playing away from 'ome, me head'd leave me shoulders, d'ya know what I mean? It ain't even werf it...

The GIRLS *tickle* MR BACON *– though lightly pleading with them to stop, he doesn't appear to be minding it too much. The* GIRLS *then begin to carry out a cute little dance routine in front of him. A distracted* MR BACON *happily watches on.*

DEBT COLLECTOR 1 *and* DEBT COLLECTOR 2 *make their way over to* MR BACON *and stand behind him.*

DEBT COLLECTOR 1. Bacon?

MR BACON. Yeah.

DEBT COLLECTOR 2. Parsley Bacon?

MR BACON (*rolling his eyes*). Yeh, whatcha want?

DEBT COLLECTOR 2. Got a message for ya.

MR BACON. From 'oo?

DEBT COLLECTOR 1. Tony.

MR BACON. Tony? (*Turning round them.*) Who's To– oh shit!

DEBT COLLECTOR 2 *grabs* MR BACON – *they begin to beat him up. The* GIRLS *run away, screaming.* MR BACON *lies on the floor, hurt.*

DEBT COLLECTOR 1. Nah, nah – that is very rude. We've come all this way to see ya, and nah ya tryna run away from us?

DEBT COLLECTOR 2. Didn't even offer us a cuppa tea.

MR BACON (*in pain*). Tell Tony, I'm sorry.

DEBT COLLECTOR 1. 'Sorries' don't pay debts –

DEBT COLLECTOR 2. Sorry.

MR BACON. I'll gives ya a bit today – a fiver.

DEBT COLLECTOR 2. That all ya got?!

DEBT COLLECTOR 1. Shouldn'tchu be raking it in, son?

DEBT COLLECTOR 2 (*teasing*). I fink someone's bin a naughty boy.

DEBT COLLECTOR 1. Tell ya wot, go and fetch us the money, but if you take more than one minute, we're gonna come in.

MR BACON, *holding his ribs, slowly gets up and makes his way over to the door.*

DEBT COLLECTOR 1. Chop-chop!

MR BACON, *with his orders, now shuffles quickly over to stage door, and heads on in.*

After a short time, MR BACON *opens the door, and hands* DEBT COLLECTOR 2 *a wad of notes. He counts them and,*

ACT ONE, SCENE FOUR   31

having found there to be the exact sum, signals to DEBT COLLECTOR 1 *that it's time to leave.*

DEBT COLLECTOR 2 (*smirking*). See ya next week, *Parsley.* (*Winks.*)

MR BACON *shuts the door.* DEBT COLLECTOR 1 *and* DEBT COLLECTOR 2 *exit through the yard.*

Enter a determined JOANNA *from the yard, carrying a smallish, rather worn-looking suitcase. She passes the* DEBT COLLECTORS *but does not acknowledge them.* JOANNA *walks straight over to stage door and knocks.* MR BACON *quickly answers it. He now has blood coming from his lip.*

JOANNA (*concerned*). Oh my gawd! Are you al/right?

MR BACON (*fearfully looking about for the* DEBT COLLECTORS). / 'Oo are you? Wot d'ya want?

JOANNA. Joanna Morris. I've come to see *the Great Batwa.*

MR BACON. Last night was the last of the tour.

JOANNA. I know. I saw it. Is he 'ere?

MR BACON. Why, do you know 'im?

JOANNA. No. I've come to save 'im.

MR BACON (*not even acknowledging what she's just said*). Okay, 'e's just collecting his fings, he'll be out in a sec.

MR BACON *slams the door shut.*

Unfazed, JOANNA *places her suitcase centre-stage and sits on it. She waits.*

A short moment later we hear the sound of male voices and laughter from behind the door. JOANNA *quickly stands, and picks up her case – she's ready. The stage door opens. First to come through it is* COLONEL HARRIS, *no longer in explorer/safari attire, he is dressed in a smart suit and top hat. He is followed by* BATWA, *again no longer in a grass skirt, but dressed in a smart, sharp-tailored suit, derby hat, spectacles and expensive shoes.* JOANNA*'s jaw drops open; she stands there unapologetically gawping.*

MR BACON *appears. It would seem from their demeanour that the three are the best of friends.* MR BACON *hands* COLONEL HARRIS *an envelope full of cash.* COLONEL HARRIS *peers into the envelope, smiles, and places the envelope in his jacket pocket.* COLONEL HARRIS *and* BATWA *both shake* MR BACON's *hand,* MR BACON *shuts the door.* COLONEL HARRIS *and* BATWA, *marking the corners and the edge of the stage, exit through the yard stage-left.*

JOANNA *stares at* BATWA *the entire time as he cheerfully makes his way past her.*

With BATWA *and* COLONEL HARRIS *having exited,* JOANNA *looks the audience dead in the eye.* JOANNA *takes a breath, goes to speak, but realises she doesn't really know what to say – and so suddenly dashes off to follow* BATWA.

Quickly realising she's forgotten her suitcase, JOANNA *turns, comes back for it, and runs off as fast as she can after him.*

Scene Five

Enter BATWA *and* COLONEL HARRIS *from the yard stage-right.* JOANNA, *still with suitcase in hand, stealthily follows from a distance. As* COLONEL HARRIS *reaches the centre-stage doors and is preoccupied with finding the right key,* BATWA *turns to discreetly talk to* JOANNA.

BATWA. Go away.

COLONEL HARRIS *unlocks the door.*

JOANNA (*confused*). Hang abaat... do you speak English??

COLONEL HARRIS. Batwa!

ACT ONE, SCENE FIVE 33

COLONEL HARRIS *enters the house, leaving the door open.* BATWA *runs over to the door.*

JOANNA (*pleading*). Mr Batwa, sir, please, me name is Joanna Morris, and I saw your pygmy show last night.

BATWA *looks at* JOANNA *before slamming the door shut.*

JOANNA *dashes over to the door, and knocks.*

Enter a BOBBY, *who spots* JOANNA *seemingly behaving strangely and stands watching her.*

Mr Batwa. It would be really good to talk to you abaat it, like, abaat like why it is you're nah wearing proper shoes 'n' nat –

JOANNA *knocks again.*

Mr Batwa, yeah, I'm not being funny, but I've come all this way to see yer, and so the least you could do is open the door. Please.

JOANNA *knocks again for a period of time. Out of the corner of her eye she suddenly spots the* BOBBY, *and so turns to him and freezes.*

BOBBY. Everyfing alright?

Beat.

JOANNA (*thinking on her feet*). Yeah. He's me pal so...

Beat.

BOBBY. Carry on.

The BOBBY *exits.* JOANNA *watches him go.*

A thought comes to JOANNA, *she looks at the door and begins to sing.*

Song – 'He's me pal' by Ada Jones

JOANNA.
I know a lad and when I feel bad
He drives all me troubles away

A CHIMNEY SWEEP *throws a coin at* JOANNA *he passes.*

Oh, thank you.

When he's your friend, he's yours to the end
No matter what others may say
He don't tell me how I ought to be

BISCUIT LADY *throws a coin at* JOANNA *as she passes.*

Ta!

He likes me just as I am
So, when I gets blue

NURSE *passes* JOANNA.

NURSE. Give it a rest, love!

JOANNA. **He's the one I go to**
For his heart is as big as a ham

JOANNA *then loudly sings and dances around the stage with great gusto. As she does, enter a flurry of Southend residents, including* – STRONG MAN, SCHOOL TEACHER, MOTHER WITH BABY IN PRAM, CHIMNEY SWEEP, NURSE *and* BISCUIT LADY.

As they enter, the townspeople stare. Is this woman mad or possessed?

He's me pal, he's me pal
There ain't nobody else I can see

COLONEL (*from behind the door*). Batwa! BATWA! Shut that woman up!

JOANNA.
I know he's dead tough
but his love ain't no bluff
He'd share his last dollar with me

BATWA *opens the door, and marches over to* JOANNA.

BATWA. Stop it! Please stop it!

JOANNA. I'll stop it when you let me in.

COLONEL (*speaking from behind the door*). Batwa!

JOANNA *continues humming the tunes loudly and dancing.*

SCHOOLTEACHER. We expect better round these parts.

BATWA. Yes of course, sir, but –

SCHOOLTEACHER *exits.*

MOTHER WITH BABY IN PRAM*'s baby bursts out crying, and so she tries her best to quieten the baby down.*

Enter COUSIN ARTHUR (*the world's most boring man*) *with a telegram. He makes his way to Batwa's front door, knocks and waits.*

MOTHER WITH BABY IN PRAM (*soothingly*). There, there darlin', the mad lady and 'er best friend don't mean it.

Exit MOTHER WITH BABY IN PRAM.

BATWA (*imploring*). Madam, really, she is not my friend.

JOANNA *continues to sing:*

JOANNA.
He's de best ever wuz
And I loves him because
He's me pal, he's me pal!
He's me pal, he's me pal!

Enter suddenly, through the centre stage door, COLONEL HARRIS, *dressed in a kimono with a large-barrelled gun in hand.*

COLONEL HARRIS (*annoyed*). BATWA!!!

He aims the gun at COUSIN ARTHUR. COUSIN ARTHUR *doesn't react.*

Any remaining townspeople (except COUSIN ARTHUR*) quickly exit.*

(*Exclaiming.*) Good Lord, it's the postman! What do *you* want?!

COUSIN ARTHUR *(holding out the telegram)*. Telegram.

COLONEL HARRIS *lowers the gun.* COUSIN ARTHUR *exits.*

COLONEL HARRIS. Much obliged to you, sir! *(Opens the telegram and begins to read it.)* Don't mind me… OH POLLOCKS!!!!!

COLONEL HARRIS *quickly steps inside the door, slams it shut and – in a flash – reappears again with his kimono off and safari hat on. He's ready to go.*

BATWA *(anxiously)*. Wait. Please. What is it? Where are you going? Shall I come with you?

COLONEL HARRIS. No need, Batwa, me old cobber – won't take long. Bloody Belgian bureaucrats are playing silly buggers again with our Congo permits.

BATWA. But you're still taking me home??

COLONEL HARRIS. Yes, nothing to worry about – *(Realising it might be a problem.)* just need to speak to a few rich and powerful friends of mine and we'll be off next week as promised.

BATWA. You promise?

COLONEL HARRIS. I promise.

As COLONEL HARRIS *goes to exit,* BATWA *looks at* JOANNA.

BATWA. Wait! When will you back?

COLONEL HARRIS. As soon as I can. Look – *(Taking* BATWA *by the hand.)* I'll miss you too, old boy, really – in the meantime – *(Spotting* JOANNA.*)* you girl!

JOANNA. Who, me?

COLONEL HARRIS. Yes, you. Who else? Do you have a job?

JOANNA. No.

COLONEL HARRIS. Want one?

JOANNA. Yeh.

COLONEL HARRIS. Excellent. Then take good care of this man here for me; be his keeper. Money's on the side. I expect to hear wonderful things when I get back.

COLONEL HARRIS *begins to leave for the yard.*

BATWA. But –

COLONEL HARRIS (*insisting*). Batwa, *relax*. You're at the *seaside*; have an ice cream, stroll the pier, I'll be back before you know it!

COLONEL HARRIS *quickly dashes through the yard.*

BATWA *glares at* JOANNA. *He then makes his way over and enters, leaving it ajar.* JOANNA *toddles over to the door; she smiles at the audience before closing it.*

Scene Six

Enter MR BACON *through the stage-right door with his clothes a tad dishevelled, blood on his lip, a black eye and a bandaged hand. He is being followed by* MRS BACON *and* HARRIET, *their maid, who carries a chair.* HARRIET *places the chair down-centre and exits stage-right.*

MRS BACON (*placing the chair down*). Right, sit daan!

MR BACON. I slipped.

MRS BACON (*with authority*). Sit daan!

MR BACON *remains standing.*

If you don't sit daan, I'll fink you don't love me.

MR BACON *sits.* MRS BACON *tenderly looks at his wounds.*

You fink I was born yesterday, don't cha?

MR BACON *remains silent.*

'Ow much trouble we in?

MR BACON. You ain't in any, I am.

MRS BACON (*snappy*). I said, 'How much trouble *we* in?', didn't I?

Beat.

MR BACON (*ashamed*). A lot.

MRS BACON (*in shock*). My God, Parsley –

MR BACON (*justifying*). Well 'ow else dya fink it got to be '*The largest entertainment building in Europe*'??

MRS BACON (*realising*). My God, Parsley, if that building goes unda – what it would mean for the taan – for the people – we'd be outcasts.

MR BACON. –

MRS BACON (*a thought comes to her*). What abaat the council?

MR BACON. What about 'em?

MRS BACON. Well can't they do sunink?

MR BACON (*despairingly*). Like what? They spend most of the time arguing amongst 'emselves.

MRS BACON. What about the mayor? I'm sure he'd understand.

MR BACON. Understand wot? That me farver was a fruiter, and that, somehow, the likes of me managed to land this job? No – people like 'im are just waiting for people like to us to make mistakes.

MRS BACON. But he needs ya. It's because of you and wot you've done for that building, 'e woz re-elected.

The doorbell rings.

(*Taking charge.*) You're scared, Parsley, I get that –

The doorbell rings again.

I am too.

The door bell rings again.

HARRIET!

We see HARRIET *quickly enter and make her way over to stage-left. She shoves a piece of paper into her apron pocket – a Suffragette newsletter.*

(*Returning to her conversation with her husband.*) But I believe in ya – ain't like we ain't 'ad dark times before. Times when there seemed no light, when the silence in this 'ouse was overbearing.

So, you listen to me –

(*Taking his hands, she speaks gently to him.*) You are, wivaat a doubt, the stupidest man I 'av evva met or will evva meet, but my God, I love you wiv every ounce of my being, and I ain't losing ya wivaat a fight, do you 'ear me? So –

Enter HARRIET, *holding a chair. She doesn't knock, instead she enters with a great burst of excitement. She is followed by* MAYOR INGRAM *and* VIOLET.

HARRIET (*announcing the guests as though this were a grand ball*). Presenting, His Royal Highness, the Mayor of Saffend-on-Sea, and 'is daughter – (*Quickly turning to* VIOLET.) What's your name again?

VIOLET. Violet May / Ingram –

HARRIET (*shouting*). / Lady Violet!

MRS BACON (*wincing*). Harriet, would you kindly bring us some cake?

MAYOR INGRAM (*excitedly*). Very kind of you, Mrs / Bacon.

VIOLET. / Not for me, I'm watching my figure.

HARRIET *curtsies, puts the chair down and exits.*

MRS BACON. Do forgive the maid, she's new – won't you take a seat, Mr Mayor? Violet?

MAYOR INGRAM *and* VIOLET *sit.*

MAYOR INGRAM *spots* MR BACON*'s injuries.*

MAYOR INGRAM. I say, Bacon, everything alright?

Having forgotten his dishevelled appearance, MR BACON *quickly makes himself more presentable, e.g. tucking his shirt in and smoothing his hair over.*

MR BACON (*embarrassed*). Yes, sir – I rather foolishly slipped over earlier – done meself in good and propa.

MAYOR INGRAM. Yes, I can see. (*Taking charge.*) Now, Bacon, I've been thinking – (*Bottling it.*) How's the ice rink coming along?

MR BACON. Good, sir, thank you, woz an excellent idea of yours.

VIOLET *gently clears her throat – a signal to her father to move the conversation along.*

MAYOR INGRAM. Yes quite. Now, Bacon, I was wondering if we might be able to have a little chat – man to man – and Violet, of course.

MRS BACON *raises her eyebrows.* MR BACON *winces – he knows his wife won't take to kindly to the request.*

MRS BACON (*calmly*). With the greatest of respect, Mr Mayor, I fink you'll find *you've* come into to *my* 'ouse…

MAYOR INGRAM (*feeling put in his place*). Er – yes quite.

MRS BACON. So may I enquire, as to what it is Your Honour would like to talk to my husband abaat?

MAYOR INGRAM (*embarrassed*). Of course, and forgive me, Bacon, but, what with this news of Folkestone –

Frustrated with her father taking so long, VIOLET *takes over the conversation.*

VIOLET. Oh for heaven's sake! (*Speaking rather quickly.*) Look – Cordelia said to Iris, who said to Winnie, who said to Agatha, who said to Beryl, who said to Audrey, who said to Maggie, who said to Maisie, who said to Tillie, who said to Ruth, who said to me, that it might be an idea for us to hold an international beauty pageant of our own, here at the Kursaal.

HARRIET *squeals.* MR BACON, MRS BACON, MAYOR INGRAM *and* VIOLET *all look at her.*

HARRIET. Don't mind me.

HARRIET *takes a slice of cake, shoves it in her mouth and eats it.* MR BACON *slowly returns his gaze to* MAYOR INGRAM.

MR BACON. Look, I'm sorry, Mayor, but I just don't fink there's anything gained by us doing one. The cost alone would / be –

VIOLET (*throwing a tantrum*). / Daddy!

MAYOR INGRAM. Surely money's no issue for the Kursaal, Bacon??

MR BACON (*excusing*). Plus, I don't *really* know what a pageant is anyway. I mean I do, but like, not what the girls actually *do* in 'em? Like, *actually* do exactly?

VIOLET (*excitedly*). Dress up, put on their best frocks –

MR BACON. And...?

VIOLET. Wear fancy shoes, style their hair –

HARRIET (*speaking with her mouth full*). – wash their face –

MR BACON. – and then what?

VIOLET *ponders.*

VIOLET (*thinking out loud*). Do you know, I honestly don't know. Haven't the foggiest.

Beat.

But it all sounds jolly good fun!

MR BACON (*with raised eyebrows*). Does it?!

HARRIET (*matter-of-fact*). You know, some say the Beauty pageant's origin lies in the *English May Day* celebrations, and the choosing of one woman to serve as a symbol of a community's beautification ideals and values.

MR BACON (*pondering*). I don't know…?

VIOLET (*throwing a tantrum*). DADDY!!!!

MAYOR INGRAM (*authoritatively*). Look, Bacon –

VIOLET (*throwing a tantrum*). DADDY!!!!

MAYOR INGRAM. Violet says it sold out.

MR BACON (*surprised*). 'Sold aat'??

MAYOR INGRAM (*pleading*). Yes.

MR BACON. What abaat next year??

VIOLET. No one will care about beauty pageants next year! It has be *now*! DADDY!!

MAYOR INGRAM (*suggestively*). Next weekend? What do you think?

MRS BACON (*taking charge*). D'ya know wot I fink? I fink we should all calm daan a moment? Take a little breff?

Nah, Mr Mayor – *if*, and let's be honest, it is an 'if' at this point – *if* my 'usband were to arrange an *international beauty pageant* at the Kursaal, a big one, last minute and that – sunink we – (*Correcting herself.*) he ain't ever done before, sunink that perhaps might not have made its way into this year's budget, what with the ice rink and that, I'm sure you'd appreciate that a little 'elp, just to get us – (*Correcting herself.*) him, started, would go a long way.

He'd of course wanna do it proper. The Kursaal fits, what? Four thousand people? That's a lot. I doubt – sold aat or not – Folkestone's pageant will be seen by anywhere near that number. And so *if* he were to do it, you wouldn't want him to get it wrong? Not in front of *all* them people. And so what

ACT ONE, SCENE SIX 43

abaat a trip to Folkestone for 'im – to check aat the pageant, because then, and only then, does Southend 'av *any* chance of beatin' those idiots across the water.

Course, it goes without sayin' that this all comes at a personal cost; the first-class train ticket alone would cost a small fortune, plus he'd 'av to 'av lodgings – nice ones mind, food, drink, and a whole new wardrobe –

MR BACON (*softly*). I don't need a whole new wardrobe, luv?

Without looking at him, MRS BACON *gestures for* MR BACON *to not interrupt.*

MRS BACON. *PLUS* – and a little sunink extra – plus tax, of course, you wouldn't want 'im aat of pocket wouldcha, Mr Mayor? 'Ow's all that sound?

MAYOR INGRAM. Well –

VIOLET (*trying to hold her anger in*). Daddy, please!! Mummy will be turning in her grave!

MRS BACON (*chirpily*). Could get the final figure to you as soon as this afternoon – if you think that would 'elp, Mayor?

Beat.

MAYOR INGRAM (*somewhat hesitant*). Yes – I think we could accommodate all of that… if you think it would help, Bacon?

MR BACON. It certainly would, sir.

HARRIET. I'd love to enter a beauty pageant, can I come?

MR BACON *and* MRS BACON. No!

MRS BACON. No working-class girls allowed.

HARRIET (*insulted*). Charming.

MAYOR INGRAM (*rising from his chair*). Well, Violet and I won't take up any more of your time.

HARRIET opens the stage-left door. MAYOR INGRAM *and* VIOLET *make their way over to the door.*

VIOLET (*suddenly turning around*). Wait! Did I mention that the best-looking gal gets a crown??

HARRIET. No, you didn't.

VIOLET *smirks before exiting.*

MR BACON (*offering his hand*). Take care, Mr Mayor.

MAYOR INGRAM (*shaking* MR BACON*'s hand*). Mr Bacon – Mrs Bacon – good day.

Exit MAYOR INGRAM, *followed by* HARRIET.

MRS BACON (*smiling*). Yes it is.

MRS BACON *looks to her husband.*

MR BACON (*with a smirk*). Mrs Bacon… What you up to?

MRS BACON *draws* MR BACON *near to her and the two passionately kiss.* MRS BACON *then takes her husband by the the hand, and leads him off through one of the centre stage doors. Their giddiness implies they are heading up to the bedroom.*

Scene Seven

Enter JOANNA *through the stage-right door. In great haste she sweeps the floor, sets the chairs, and dusts the stage-left pillar.*

Enter BATWA *through the stage-right door.* JOANNA *pops out from behind the stage-left pillar, unintentionally making* BATWA *jump. He makes to leave.*

JOANNA (*calling after him*). Wait! You're gonna aff to talk to us some time.

BATWA *stops.*

(*Gently.*) I've said I'm sorry and I am, truly. I shouldn't 'av done wot I did, but I can't change it.

BATWA. –

JOANNA. I can't change it, can I?

Beat.

BATWA. What do you want?

JOANNA. Just to talk.

BATWA. About what?

JOANNA. Abaat you – (*Referring to his clothes.*) this – I'd come to save yer.

BATWA (*insulted*). 'Save me'?

JOANNA. Yes, I'd come to save ya from the colonel.

BATWA. From my friend?

JOANNA (*confused*). Yes. And from this life.

BATWA. Save *me*?

JOANNA *stares at* BATWA *for a moment.*

JOANNA (*trying her best to hold in her annoyance*). Nah why do I get the sense that you're being a tad prickly with me, when maybe I'm the one who should be being prickly with you.

BATWA. 'Prickly'?

JOANNA. Yeah, English, for 'touchy' – you got any uvva questions? – Okay then, I'll ask some –

BATWA. You are angry.

JOANNA (*angry*). Yes I'm angry. I'm angry at *you*. Because of yer little charade last night, I'm now finking fings I ain't never fought before. I'm 'aving rows with people I ain't never rowed with and all because I felt sorry for ya.

BATWA *laughs.*

Is sunink funny?

BATWA *laughs again.*

D'ya fancy sharing it wida resta the class?

BATWA. I feel sorry for *you*.

JOANNA (*rather taken aback*). For *me*??

BATWA. Yes, for you. You are a yellow woman in a white world.

JOANNA (*becoming angry*). 'Yellow'? Hang abaat! I ain't yellow!

BATWA. Your skin, it's yellow. You're a half-caste.

JOANNA. Yes I know that but – *Wait a minute*. This ain't even abaat me, this is abaat you, and you pretending to be a pygmy when you ain't?!

BATWA (*confused*). But I am. I am Batwa Douze, Chief of the Bambuti tribe; Ituri Forest, the Congo. But who, may I ask, are *you*? Other than a very annoying woman who thinks bursting in is the best way to get what she wants – but then isn't that what the British always do – apparently?

Embarrassed, JOANNA *holds her tongue.*

JOANNA. Breakfast?

JOANNA *suddenly exits stage-left.*

BATWA. I'm not hungry.

JOANNA (*from offstage*). I weren't sure of what you liked, so I just put aat a few bits –

Enter JOANNA *wheeling on a breakfast table and placing it centre-stage. On it we see a teapot, cups and saucer, cutlery, a bowl of lemon slices, two bowls of porridge, fresh bread, butter, milk, marmalade, salt, apples, and boiled eggs – it's quite the little feast.*

JOANNA *gets a chair and places it at the table. She gestures for* BATWA *to sit. He does so.*

BATWA (*kindly*). Aren't you going to join me? I won't start until you do.

JOANNA *then grabs a chair and makes her way over to the table. She sits, quickly closes her eyes and quietly says a prayer. She then tucks in – it's all absolutely delicious. As she eats, a curious* JOANNA *watches* BATWA. *She observes him at one point, putting a slice of lemon into his tea.*

BATWA (*friendly*). So, Miss Joanna, tell me about you. Where's home?

JOANNA. I dunno really.

BATWA (*confused*). How do you not know??

JOANNA. I don't know. I dunno who me mum and dad are, see –

BATWA (*realising there's been a miscommunication*). Oh.

JOANNA. 'Ow I really ended up 'ere. But I've always imagined –

From the yard enters JOANNA'S MUM; *a white working-class, cockney woman, and* JOANNA'S MUM'S FRIEND. *They are giggling away and having the time of their lives.*

– that one summer, me mum, along with a mate of 'ers, came daan to Southend for a bit of bank 'oliday fun, and that that evening, they headed to what would have been the King's Hall, Westcliff, to hear the band play.

Onto Juliet's balcony emerges JOANNA'S DAD; *a music-hall, African drummer; a black man dressed in a suit that has seen better days. He plays as though it's the only thing he was born to do.*

We see JOANNA'S MUM *mesmerised by* JOANNA'S DAD *and so stands watching him. She grips her chest, she's never seen anything or anyone so beautiful in all her life. She turns to her friend, and* JOANNA'S MUM'S FRIEND *knowingly nods and exits.*

– and that it was there that Dad caught me mum's eye – 'e was African, I reckon, so a drummer? – and finking he was a bit of alright, me mum probs hung around after the show to 'av words.

Enter JOANNA'S DAD *onto the stage through the SL door.*

The two talk. It's TOWIE meets 'Classic Hollywood' in style. As JOANNA *speaks the following lines, she lovingly watches the vision of her mum and dad.*

JOANNA *and* JOANNA'S MUM *(flirty but friendly)*. Oi oi, drummer boy.

JOANNA. She goes.

JOANNA *and* JOANNA'S DAD *(confused)*. Are you talking to me?

JOANNA. 'E sez.

JOANNA'S MUM *(teasingly)*. Well there ain't no one else round 'ere, is there?

JOANNA'S DAD *(teasingly)*. If I'm not mistaken, madam, are you trying to woo me?

JOANNA'S MUM. What if I am?

JOANNA'S DAD. Have we met before?

JOANNA'S MUM. No, we ain't. But I saw you just nah in ya show, and every beat you played spoke to me, you know? I ain't eva 'eard music that beautiful before.

JOANNA'S DAD *(sincerely)*. I think you're beautiful.

JOANNA'S MUM. Are you tryna woo *me* now?

JOANNA'S DAD *(worried he's insulted her)*. Not at all –

JOANNA'S MUM. Coz you can.

JOANNA'S DAD *(smiling)*. Are English ladies always this forward?

JOANNA'S MUM. I ain't like other English ladies.

JOANNA'S DAD. No, you are not. I'm sorry to say, I'm leaving tomorrow for a place called *Clacton-on-Sea*, so I guess this is goodbye.

JOANNA'S MUM. Don't aff to be. What if, just for one night, we did what we wanted, not what the world tells us to do?

What if we made sweet love daan by the estuary under the stars?

JOANNA'S DAD. I'd like that very much.

JOANNA'S DAD makes to walk over to JOANNA'S MUM. JOANNA'S MUM suddenly gestures for him to stop.

JOANNA'S MUM. Just so you know, I don't normally do this.

JOANNA'S MUM grabs JOANNA'S DAD by the shirt, and the two kiss – it's beautifully passionate. The loving couple then run over to JOANNA and take her by the hand, they whirl her around the stage.

JOANNA (*yelling at us as though she is on a roller coaster*). And so that night they made love! Sweet, jammy love, and it was beautiful!

SUITED BAND MEMBER pops their head out of the stage-left door and whistles to JOANNA'S DAD to hurry along. JOANNA'S DAD leaves.

Few months later Mum discovered she was having us, and coz she couldn't keep me, I reckon she did the only fing that made sense. She left me in the place where it all began; a place of love: Southend-on-Sea.

Enter NUN from the yard. JOANNA'S MUM goes over to her and hands her the baby. NUN carefully takes the baby from her, and goes to walk away. JOANNA'S MUM tearfully turns away from NUN. NUN suddenly turns back.

NUN. Wait! What's her name?

Beat.

JOANNA'S MUM. Same as mine – 'Joanna'.

NUN nods and exits. Exit a tearful JOANNA'S MUM. JOANNA watches her mum leave.

BATWA brings over to JOANNA a cup of tea. JOANNA takes it and sips it.

JOANNA. So 'ow long you bin travelling round wiv the colonel then?

BATWA. Three years.

JOANNA. Free years?! Don'tcha miss 'ome?

BATWA. Yes of course but –

JOANNA. Then why don't you go back? Ain't you missing your people? Don't they miss you?

BATWA. Yes, but as chief –

JOANNA (*surprised*). Chief? You royalty?

BATWA (*coyly*). Well…

JOANNA quickly puts her tea down and curtsies..

An embarrassed BATWA helps JOANNA to her feet.

Please, no. We don't do all that.

JOANNA (*excitedly*). So what's it like being royal then?

BATWA (*thinking*). I don't know. People look at you differently. They see you. Does that make sense?

JOANNA. Not really, no. But 'ow comes you ain't treated as royal over 'ere then?

BATWA. Well over here, I guess the word 'chief', makes people nervous.

JOANNA. Is being chief 'ow come you met the King then?

BATWA suddenly seems very serious.

Forgive me, it ain't my place to ask.

BATWA. Is there anything else you want to know?

JOANNA. You mean, other than why you're tricking people aat of their money into finking you're sunink that you ain't?

BATWA (*confused*). What am I not? I am pygmy.

JOANNA (*confused*). Yeah butcha clothes ain't. You put lemon in your tea, you speak English better than I do.

BATWA. You can be more than one thing, you know.

ACT ONE, SCENE SEVEN 51

JOANNA (*pondering*). Suppose so — but 'ow can ya let the colonel go round sayin' them terrible fings abaat cha for free years?

BATWA. Currency, I suppose. In return I get see places, do things, learn things, things that I'll share with the others when I get back – things the others can only dream of. What do you dream of?

JOANNA (*surprised*). Me? You'll fink it's stupid.

BATWA (*earnestly*). I won't.

JOANNA. Well, that's part of the reason why I'm 'ere, see – This all started yesterday because of a beauty pageant.

BATWA. What is a 'beauty pageant'?

JOANNA. It's like, a competition – where girls dress up, and the prettiest one gets a crown.

BATWA (*fearfully*). A crown?!

JOANNA. Yeh, a crown. And so I says to Mrs Bugle, me mistress, I says that I'd like to enter the international beauty pageant daan in Folkestone.

BATWA. 'International'?

JOANNA (*annoyed at herself*). Yeh that's right. And I asked 'er if she fought I'd win, but she weren't having none of it. So I walked away – and nah, basically, I don't fink we can be friends no more.

A sadness comes over JOANNA.

BATWA. And why do you want to enter one?

JOANNA (*struggling to find the words*). Well, why not??

BATWA. So what stopped you?

JOANNA. From what?

BATWA. Entering the pageant in – (*Enjoying the sounds.*) *Folkestone*?

Beat.

JOANNA *slams down her cutlery.*

JOANNA (*exclaiming*). 'Ere, you're right!

BATWA. It was just a question – I'm not saying –

JOANNA (*a thought comes to her*). Nah, nah, nah – what if what 'appened with Mrs Bugle 'appened for a reason? I am – now – my own person. *Free* to do whatever I like, when I like. And what I'd like to do, no – what I am *going* to do, is to enter the Miss Folkestone 1908 Beauty Pageant.

A brave JOANNA *looks out towards the audience.*

It's gonna be cold swimming across that estuary, but I ain't scared, because people 'av always done mad fings in the name of destiny.

Beat.

BATWA (*not looking at her*). Would you like some money for the train?

JOANNA. Yes please. (*Turning back to* BATWA *and smiling.*) That's very kind of you, Mr Batwa.

BATWA. You are welcome. In that case, shall we clear up, and then we can begin to make arrangements?

JOANNA. Yes please, again, Mr Batwa. Thank you.

BATWA *nods.* JOANNA, *trying her best to hold back her obvious glee, hastily takes the two chairs off through the stage-left door.* BATWA *leaves with the breakfast table, through the stage-right door.*

Scene Eight

It's now Saturday – the day of the Folkestone beauty pageant. The event is (apparently) about to begin.

We hear a blast of music; it's upbeat, seasidy.

The centre doors open to reveal MAYOR PEPPER, PERRY, THOMAS *and* TWO MEMBERS OF THE BAND; *one plays a tuba and the other a trombone.*

MAYOR PEPPER *has his civic regalia,* THOMAS *carries a clipboard and pencil, and* PERRY *wears a sandwich board that reads, 'Miss Folkestone International Beauty Pageant 1908 – Sign up here'.* PERRY *also has, in each hand, a little Union Jack flag.*

The five enter as a group – they keep tight, with MAYOR PEPPER *at the front. The group land centre, downstage of the pillars – the music disintegrates. Silence.*

ALL *wait.*

And wait.

ALL *look around.*

And then wait some more.

THOMAS (*tentatively*). Well, Pepper, it would seem –

MAYOR PEPPER. – quiet, Thomas. They'll be here.

THOMAS (*even more tentatively*). It's just, if they're not, there are rather a lot of people waiting inside –

MAYOR PEPPER (*defiant*). Yes, I'm well aware of that. Now, remember, as soon as they're here, we'll line 'em up, weed out the most unlikely, and then the others can go backstage to prepare.

From the yard enters WOMAN NOT INTERESTED IN BEAUTY PAGEANTS 1, *a working-class woman who carries a basket of flowers.*

MAYOR PEPPER (*with great enthusiasm*). Ahh, here we go! (*Addressing the woman.*) Good day, madam! Here to apply for this afternoon's beauty pageant, are we?

WOMAN 1 (*affronted*). No! No, I *ain't*! *Ain't* nothing but a bunch of perverts!

WOMAN 1 *exits.*

PERRY (*calling after her*). Oh. No. We. *Ain't!* Ain't nothing wrong with admiring the female form!

Enter, from the other side of the yard, WOMAN NOT INTERESTED IN BEAUTY PAGEANTS 2. *An upper-class woman, she carries under her arm a small dog.*

MAYOR PEPPER (*full of charm*). Ahh, here she is, the first contestant of the after/noon!

WOMAN 2 (*aloof*). / Certainly not. One expects better of you, Mayor. To self-sabotage is one thing but to bring the whole of Folkestone down with you is quite another.

WOMAN 2 *starts to exit.*

THOMAS (*turning to the others*). Wouldn't get my vote anyway.

WOMAN 2 *turns and glares at the men. Her dog growls.*

WOMAN 2 (*speaking to her dog*). Calm, Pookie.

She exits.

PERRY (*politely insisting*). Mayor Pepper – if I may – perhaps we should consider cancelling the pageant?

Enter MR BACON *from the yard, dressed as a pageant girl. He makes no attempt whatsoever to 'act female'.*

MAYOR PEPPER (*extremely relieved to see an obvious contestant*). Ahh! Ah-ha! You seeeeee. '*Patience is a virtue*', old chap.

Welcome, madam! Welcome to Britain's first *ever* international beauty pageant!

MR BACON (*trying to seem enthusiastic*). Yeahhhhhhhhhh.

MAYOR PEPPER. Have you travelled far?

MR BACON. Just 'cross the water.

MAYOR PEPPER. France?

MR BACON. Not quite.

THOMAS. Name?

MR BACON. Parsley.

ACT ONE, SCENE EIGHT   55

THOMAS (*confused*). 'Parsley'??

MR BACON (*realising his mistake and so quickly correcting himself*). Rosemary.

PERRY (*saying her name is a dreamy manner*). '*Rosemary*'? – Fabulous!

MAYOR PEPPER. Well welcome, Rosemary – we are thrilled to have you with us, and all shall begin soon.

MR BACON. So what's the plan then? Like, wot are we gonna do? Just walk up and daan?

MAYOR PEPPER (*genuinely*). Well there's a lot more to it than that, I assure you.

MR BACON (*looking around*). So where is everyone?

Awkward pause.

THOMAS *leans into* MAYOR PEPPER.

THOMAS (*pleading*). Pepper –

PERRY (*leaning into* MAYOR PEPPER). Sir, we can't have an international beauty contest with only one British contestant, it's just not cricket.

MAYOR PEPPER *hears something in the distance.*

MAYOR PEPPER (*hushing them*). Ssh!

PERRY (*worried*). What ever is it?

MAYOR PEPPER. That sound. Do you hear it? Painful; awful, in fact. Like nails on a blackboard.

THOMAS (*straining to hear*). I think I can?

MAYOR PEPPER. Only one thing makes a noise that horrid.

ALL *look at one another, grin and say...*

MAYOR PEPPER, PERRY, THOMAS, BAND MEMBERS. GIRLS!!

From the yard emerge a stampede of PAGEANT GIRLS *including* LILIAN EDWARDS, MIRIAM CARTER, LENA SABINE KOPPENSTEINER, CATALINA MARGARITA HERNANDEZ *and* MARTINA FRANCESCA GUILIA

ISABELLA AGOSTINELLI. *They are excited, and so screaming and laughing loudly. They charge past* MAYOR PEPPER, MR BACON, PERRY *and* THOMAS, *and make their way off through the centre-stage doors. In the process,* MR BACON *is swept up by the girls and exits with them'.*

Enter JOANNA *with her suitcase from the yard.*

MAYOR PEPPER (*calling after the girls*). Girls! Girls! Please! Calm down! Calm down! In you go! That's it! Thank you, girls! Form an orderly line inside!

JOANNA. Excuse me? I'm 'ere for the beauty pageant.

ALL *turn and stare at* JOANNA.

(*Oblivious to the mood.*) Sorry I'm late – some fella went and sent us in the wrong direction. If I hadn't 'av 'eard this lot and followed 'em , I probably wouldn't 'av made it. Coz don't get me wrong, I've had a lovely time looking around Folkestone. There isn't much to see – or do – but you do do well with what you 'av – to be honest, I expected a lot worse.

MAYOR PEPPER *looks to* THOMAS *and* PERRY, *before making his way over to* JOANNA.

MAYOR PEPPER. Excuse me, miss, might you indulge me in a private word?

JOANNA. Of course – sorry again for being late – but honestly, it's only / because –

MAYOR PEPPER (*soothingly*). / Not a problem, Miss...?

JOANNA. Joanna.

JOANNA *puts her suitcase down.*

MAYOR PEPPER. Miss Joanna – (*Taking a deep breath.*) I'm afraid – and being quite honest, it is my fault entirely as I should have made it clear from the very beginning – that this afternoon we shall be unable to accept your application to the pageant.

JOANNA (*disappointed*). Coz I'm an Essex girl?

ACT ONE, SCENE EIGHT 57

MAYOR PEPPER (*awkwardly*). Not quite, you see, we have certain standards by which we like to hold ourselves accountable, and were that standard to... (*Finding the words.*) *falter... lower* to one other than what one would expect from such a public and first-of-its-kind event, it could mean that all our hard work, *hours* of preparation, risks being all for nothing. And at the end of the day, all we really want is for people to be able to enjoy themselves – both those participating, as well as those watching and, well, I'd like to think you're a woman who understands all that??

Beat.

Realising what he's saying, JOANNA *slowly picks up her suitcase. She is wounded.*

(*Relieved.*) Good! (*Quickly turning round.*) Now then, gentlemen! LET THE BEAUTY PAGEANT BEGIN!!

Exit MAYOR PEPPER, THOMAS *and* PERRY *through the centre-stage doors. The doors close behind them.*

JOANNA *makes her way to the far downstage-left corner and sits, legs dangling over into the yard.*

After a moment we see MR BACON, *along with* CATALINA, *be thrown out of the pageant by* THOMAS. *Exit an insulted* CATALINA *through the yard.*

MR BACON *dashes back to try to open the door, it's locked.*

MR BACON (*begging*). Please! Please, let us in. I'll sit quiet at the back. I won't say nuffing to no one. I just need to know the basics. Please. I can't let 'er daan again. Please.

Defeated, MR BACON *walks away, only to then suddenly turn back around and throw his heel at the door. He then goes to throw the other one, but as he raises his arm he spots* JOANNA *looking at him.*

MR BACON (*aggressively*). What you looking aat?

JOANNA. Nothing.

MR BACON *senses* JOANNA*'s sadness.*

MR BACON. You alright, luv?

JOANNA (*sad*). Yeah. You?

MR BACON (*sad*). Yeah.

> MR BACON *sits down in the far downstage-right corner, with his head in hands and his feet dangling in the yard.*

MR BACON. You got far to get 'ome?

JOANNA (*annoyed*). If you're asking '*where I am from*', I was born 'ere!

MR BACON (*mortified*). Oh no, I ain't asking that. I was genuinely just asking where ya live.

> *Beat.*

JOANNA. Southend-on-Sea.

MR BACON. *Southend-on-Sea?!* I live in Southend-on-Sea! Have we met?

> JOANNA *turns to looks at him.*

JOANNA. I don't recognise ya, miss, sorry.

> *She turns back.* MR BACON *remembers he has a wig on.*

MR BACON. Oh no, 'ere – (*Removes the wig.*) TA-DAH!!

> JOANNA *shoots him a confused look.*

I'm Bacon, Parsley Bacon, I –

MR BACON *and* JOANNA. – run the Kursaal.

JOANNA (*confused*). So 'ow comes you're wearing that?

MR BACON. Research, luv. I'm meself, meant to be doing one of these international erm… / beauty pageants.

JOANNA (*helping him out*). / Beauty pageants.

MR BACON. Fank you, daan at the Kursaal next Saturday.

JOANNA. I ain't 'eard nuffing abaat it?

MR BACON. Going in the papers tomorrow, init? So it's too late to cancel and, even if I did, the mayor would 'av me guts for garters. Though he probably will anyway because instead of being in there wiv all the goings-onz, I'm sat aat 'ere with you – no offence.

JOANNA *shrugs*.

(*Self-pitying*.) The wife's gonna kill us – to be honest, I don't know why she's wiv us anyway, I only eva seem to make fings worse.

Plus the taan's gonna be on me case – that should be fun.

JOANNA. 'Ow come?

MR BACON. Coz for the first time eva, Folkestone 'av sunink we don't.

JOANNA. What?

MR BACON. All eyes on them – but maybe it's abaat time they were seen differently?

MR BACON*'s words hit* JOANNA.

JOANNA (*thinking*). Yeh.

Enter BATWA *from upstage. Dressed in their 'Great Batwa' attire. They stand onstage looking out towards the audience.*

MR BACON. This pageant 'ere, in Folkstone, it's all just act; a *facade*. All it's doing is covering up the fact that the taan looks a bit sad –

Enter MRS BUGLE *from upstage. Only* JOANNA *sees her.* MRS BUGLE *stands next to* BATWA

JOANNA. Yeh.

MR BACON. – but then there's no law against that, is there?

MR BACON*'s words again hit* JOANNA.

JOANNA. No.

MR BACON. My problem is that I've always dreamed big –

Enter PEACHES *carrying a tiara. She makes her way onto the stage and stands the other side of* BATWA.

– but then that's 'ow come the likes of me is even running the Kursaal.

JOANNA (*distracted*). The Kursaal, yeah.

And with big buildings, can come big problems, and today's is, 'ow can I make Southend's beauty pageant –

JOANNA (*correcting him*). International beauty pageant.

MR BACON. *International* beauty pageant – yeh – bigger and better than this one, because four thousand tickets is a lot.

JOANNA *stands, gathering her thoughts.*

JOANNA. I don't know.

Exit BATWA, MRS BUGLE *and* PEACHES.

The centre doors open to reveal LENA *and* MIRIAM *being waved off by* MAYOR PEPPER.

MAYOR PEPPER (*patronisingly*). I'm so sorry, girls. Better luck next time.

An affronted LENA *and* MIRIAM *exit through the yard.* MAYOR PEPPER *returns to the pageant.* JOANNA *watches the girls leave.*

JOANNA. 'Ere d'ya know what? It's weird they call 'em '*girls*', coz they ain't, they're '*women*'.

I mean technically, if you were gonna call 'em anything, you'd think they'd at least bother to relate it to *pageant queens*, coz it's not like everyone don't know, you can't be queen without being a princess first –

She's got it! JOANNA *begins to act strangely.*

MR BACON. You alright there luv?

JOANNA *is hysterically laughing – she's like a madwoman.*

(*Panicked.*) Miss?! Are you alright, shall I get a doctor?

JOANNA (*excitedly embracing him*). Mr Bacon, I think I've got a way to bring all eyes back to the Kursaal.

MR BACON. I'm listening.

JOANNA. You got a pen and bit of paper?

MR BACON (*aware of his appearance*). Well not on me luv, no, why?

JOANNA. Because I'm gonna need to write a letta.

MR BACON. To who??

JOANNA. The Mayor of Southend.

MR BACON (*surprised*). Ingram? Whatchu wanna write to him for?!

JOANNA. Because if today's taught me anyfing, I don't fink I can do – what I'm gonna do wivaat him.

MR BACON (*inquisitively*). This idea of yours, you're certain it'll work??

JOANNA (*looking him dead in the eye*). I'm certain it will, if you 'elp me.

Beat.

MR BACON (*with a smirk*). You fancy catching the train back together? You ever ridden first class?

JOANNA (*staggered*). No, I ain't.

MR BACON. It's 'Joanna', init?

JOANNA (*surprised he remembered*). Yes, it is, Mr Bacon.

Beat.

MR BACON *holds out his hand for* JOANNA *to shake. She takes it, and they do.* MR BACON *then takes a deep breath.*

MR BACON. Right then, let's getcha that ticket.

MR BACON *gestures for* JOANNA *to walk in front of him; she does so. They both exit through the yard.*

Scene Nine

It's now 3 o'clock, in the early hours.

A clock rings out across Southend-on-Sea, before striking three times.

We are in the Council Chamber of Southend-on-Sea Town Hall.

Through the stage-left door will eventually shuffle several mumbling, grumbling, yawning TOWN COUNCILLORS. *They are dressed half in pyjamas, half suited and booted – think nightcaps and neckerchiefs, nightgowns and top hats. Clearly they didn't have time to dress themselves accordingly. It's dark. There is an air of conspiracy. Some carry candles. What the hell was so important that it couldn't wait?*

Enter ROBERT.

ROBERT (*loud whisper*). Hello??

Enter CLIVE. *He stops by the door and squints at* ROBERT.

ROBERT. Clive, is that you?? I can barely see a thing.

CLIVE. Of course it's me, Robert. (*Very confused.*) Why can't we turn the lights on again?

ROBERT. He specifically said not to.

Enter GEOFFREY.

GEOFFREY. Good morning, gentlemen!

ROBERT *and* CLIVE. Geoffrey.

Enter RALPH.

RALPH. Morning, gentlemen!

CLIVE, ROBERT *and* GEOFFREY. Ralph.

Enter CECIL.

CECIL. Morning, gentlemen.

CLIVE, ROBERT, GEOFFRY, *and* RALPH. Cecil.

Enter BERNARD.

BERNARD. Morning, gentlemen.

CLIVE, ROBERT, GEOFFREY, RALPH *and* CECIL. Bernard.

Enter REGINALD *who slams the door behind him.*

CLIVE, ROBERT, GEOFFREY, RALPH, CECIL *and* BERNARD. Morning Regin/ald

ACT ONE, SCENE NINE 63

REGINALD. / WHAT THE FUCK IS GOING ON?!

BERNARD (*begging*). Reg, please – Jim wouldn't have called an emergency meeting if it wasn't important.

RALPH (*a touch of excitement*). I wonder what it's about? What couldn't have waited until morning?

REGINALD. I'll give his *lordship* two bloody minutes, and if he doesn't arrive by then I'm pissing off.

ROBERT (*sarcastically*). Oh what a surprise!

REGINALD. What do you mean by that?

ROBERT. I mean, it's not like you, Reg, to do the bare minimum.

ROBERT *and* REGINALD *square up to one another and begin engage in a game of fisticuffs. The others mumble disapprovingly.*

GEOFFREY (*trying to defuse the situation*). Oh Reg, Robert – do stop it! Please!

Suddenly the door opens. ALL *stop. Enter* MR BACON.

REGINALD. Bacon?! What in God's name are you doing here?

As MR BACON *goes to speak, enter* MAYOR INGRAM. *Just like the others, he too is dressed in suit attire with a hint of pyjamas, and of course, his civic regalia (necklace).*

MAYOR INGRAM (*calmly*). He's with me.

REGINALD *and* ROBERT *look rather sheepish.*

RALPH (*nervously*). Ingram, forgive us – (*Correcting himself.*) er – me, specifically, but what on earth is all this about?

BERNARD. I can only think that whatever it is must be terribly troublesome.

MAYOR INGRAM (*sincere*). Oh it is.

BERNARD (*scared*). Good heavens.

MAYOR INGRAM. It most certainly is.

BERNARD. I'm scared.

MAYOR INGRAM. You should be scared, Bernard.

Beat.

We all should.

ALL, *except* MR BACON, *look around at each other and mumble words of worry.*

GEOFFREY. Pray – tell us. (*Remembering* MR BACON *is present*.) And why is Bacon here? He isn't a member of the Town Council?

MAYOR INGRAM. Quite right, Geoffrey, he isn't. (*Turning to* MR BACON.) Mr Bacon? I wonder, would you kindly explain to our friends here, about the letter you received today, the letter which you brought to my house and to my attention late this evening.

MAYOR INGRAM *gestures for* MR BACON *to step forward and address the group.* MR BACON *does as he is told.*

MR BACON (*addressing* MAYOR INGRAM). Of course, Mr Mayor. (*Addressing* TOWN COUNCILLORS.) Your honours – around seven this evening like, I was 'avin me dinner – nuffing special mind, when blow me –

We hear two knocks on a door.

There goes a knock at the door, and who was it?

Beat.

CLIVE. Who??

MR BACON. Me cousin Arfur

Enter ARTHUR *who walks to downstage-centre and faces the audience.*

Lovely fella – just very boring –

MAYOR INGRAM. Hurry up.

ACT ONE, SCENE NINE   65

MR BACON. You see Arfur is also me postman, and there 'e was standing at me door with a surprise behind his back – I could tell coz he 'ad a stupid look on 'is face.

'*What is it?*', I says.

COUSIN ARTHUR. I've got sunink for you.

MR BACON. '*What? Some post?*', I goes.

COUSIN ARTHUR. Yeh. How d'ya know that?

MR BACON. '*Coz you're me postman, you twonk.*'

CECIL. '*Twonk*'??

MR BACON. 'Idiot.'

CECIL. Right.

MR BACON. '*Why didn't you just pop it through me hole?*'

COUSIN ARTHUR. Because this is special, Parsley. I ain't seen nuffin like this before.

MR BACON. – and then before you know it, he only goes and places in me 'and –

Reaching into his pocket he retrieves an envelope with zebra stripes on it and holds it high in the air.

THIS!

A communal gasp from all the COUNCILLORS. *Exit* COUSIN ARTHUR.

RALPH. Good grief! It's a… it's a letter.

GEOFFREY. And we're here because of what the letter said? That is right, isn't it, Ingram?

MAYOR INGRAM. Quite right, Geoff, yes.

ROBERT. Well then…! What did the letter say?! Who was it from?!

MAYOR INGRAM. A princess.

CLIVE. What's her name??

MR BACON. Princess Dinubolu.

CLIVE. Never heard of her.

BERNARD. What does she want?

MAYOR INGRAM. Well it seems, gentlemen, news travels fast.

REGINALD. Whatever do you mean?

MAYOR INGRAM. It would appear that Princess *Dinoboos* wishes to enter the forthcoming beauty pageant at the Kursaal.

The TOWN COUNCILLORS *all mumble.* CECIL *pipes up.*

CECIL (*confused*). So?

MAYOR INGRAM. '*So*', Cecil? What do you mean '*so*'?

CECIL. I simply mean… soooo… *do* we want her to do it…?? Or, or, we *don't*… perhaps??

He looks to Geoffrey for help.

GEOFFRY (*nervously*). I think, Ingram, what my right honourable friend here is trying to say, is that allowing this Princess type is…

MAYOR INGRAM *shakes his head slowly from left to right disapprovingly. He is implying, 'No'.*

(*Picking up on Ingram's shaking of the head.*) – *not* a good idea… for many reasons.

MAYOR INGRAM. I would agree.

CLIVE. Where's she from?

MR BACON. Senegal.

ROBERT. Senegal? – So she's a Negro?

Silence.

REGINALD. Absolutely not, I don't care if she's a princess or Queen of bloody Bongo-Bongo Land, we can't have Blacks parading around the Kursaal, we'll be the laughing stock of Britain.

ACT ONE, SCENE NINE   67

ALL (*except* MAYOR INGRAM *and* MR BACON) *jeer and shout 'Hear, hear!'*

ROBERT (*firmly*). And I'm sorry, but 'International' does not mean 'Negro'. And what kind of a message would we be sending to the rest of the country, that our great town permits such tomfoolery.

CLIVE. And if we say yes to her, then mark my words, others will come and before you know it, this town will be absolutely swarming with them.

RALPH. '*Them*'?

CLIVE. Oh Ralph, get off your high horse, you know exactly what and who I mean.

BERNARD. What if she wins?

They all laugh.

I mean it gentlemen, what if she wins?

REGINALD (*laughing*). She won't. She can't.

CLIVE. What about putting a *colour-bar* in place? I've heard they're all the rage at the moment.

Mumbles of agreement from all.

RALPH. Right then, than settles it. Bacon, you have our permission to put a colour-bar in place until this whole charade goes away.

The TOWN COUNCILLORS *shake hands – it's been a good morning's work.*

MAYOR INGRAM (*calmly*). *Gentlemen*, I don't think you quite understand the gravity of the situation.

GEOFFREY. What do you mean, Ingram?

MAYOR INGRAM. Ask yourselves, '*Who* owns *Senegal?*'

GEOFFREY. Not us Brits, that's for sure.

MAYOR INGRAM. Then who does Senegal belong to?

ALL *wince*.

BERNARD. Christ!

CLIVE. The French.

CECIL. Poodle-shaggers.

MAYOR INGRAM. So, let's think about this. If we, the town council, say no, and reject the Senegalese princess's application to enter the *Miss Southend 1908 Beauty Pageant*, then our decision could lead to a disagreement of sorts between Britain and France.

ROBERT. And?

MAYOR INGRAM. *And* with all this international rubbish floating about, you know who'd be most upset with us for upsetting the French, of all people.

The penny drops for them all, except MR BACON.

CLIVE. My God…!

MAYOR INGRAM. Him and his bloody –

ALL *except* MR BACON (*taking the mic, in French accents*). Entente Cordial.

CECIL. So '*yes*'? We are saying yes then?!!

RALPH. No, never.

ROBERT. I didn't fight in the Boer War so this great country could –

RALPH (*panicking*). The people of this town will never forgive us!

REGINALD. You know what happened the last time –

CLIVE. Of course we do, but it was a baby, a novelty, hardly threatening, and it was an ugly little thing.

An argument breaks out amongst the COUNCILLORS.

MR INGRAM. Gentlemen! Please! There is one thing we could do.

CLIVE. Tell us, Ingram.

MAYOR INGRAM. Well, I just wonder if *we* need to make the decision at all. I mean, yes of course a decision does need to be made, but what if it's not *us* that make it.

GEOFFREY (*confused*). What do you mean? We're the Town council, as voted for by the great men of / Southend

MAYOR INGRAM (*aggressively*). / BLAH, BLAH, BLAH – YES I KNOW GEOFFREY! (*Calming himself.*) I guess what I'm saying, is that we are damned if we do or don't.

Beat.

So what if *we* don't decide on the matter at all?

Everyone in the chamber is very confused.

CECIL. Then, Ingram, who would??

ALL *except* MAYOR INGRAM *slowly turn to look at* MR BACON.

MAYOR INGRAM. (*Looking out towards the audience*) The King.

MR BACON (*shocked*). The King?!

Guffaws of laughter from the TOWN COUNCILLORS.

REGINALD. Surely he's got better things to do than –

MAYOR INGRAM. BETTER THINGS TO DO THEN PREVENT A WAR BETWEEN BRITAIN AND FRANCE?!

Silence.

BERNARD. I suppose it wouldn't hurt to ask.

GEOFFREY. I'll send a telegram to Buckingham Palace right away!

CECIL. I'll come with you!

Exit GEOFFREY *and* CECIL *through the stage-left door.*

RALPH. And then *we'd* just be doing whatever the King decided, wouldn't we?

MAYOR INGRAM. Like pawns –

Exit RALPH *and* REGINALD.

CLIVE. Meaning whatever happens, *we* wouldn't really be to blame – would we?

MAYOR INGRAM *shrugs. Exit* CLIVE *and* ROBERT.

BERNARD. But it is late, Ingram, aren't you worried we'll wake him up?

MAYOR INGRAM. Oh, he'll be awake.

BERNARD (*smirking*). Of course.

BERNARD *bows and scuttles off, followed by* MR BACON.

MAYOR INGRAM (*clasping his hands together*). Goodnight, gentlemen. Sleep well. Now all we can do is wait.

Exit MAYOR INGRAM.

Scene Ten

Suddenly a large flag with the crest of Edward VII is thrust over the balcony – it hangs over the centre-stage doors.

The central doors open, to reveal KING EDWARD VII *being wheeled out on his sex chair by* COURTIER. *It's around 4 a.m. The party is still going on. There's always a party happening in Buckingham Palace.* COURTIERS – *men, women, all – enter. It's just one big, royal orgy.*

Spoken word / song – 'Dirty Bertie'

EDWARD VII.
Mummy never wanted me
She thought I was a brat
She blamed me for Daddy's death
Though I've nothing to do with that

We went for a stroll in the cold
To have a man-to-man chat

ENSEMBLE.
Naughty boy!

EDWARD VII.
It's not my fault he caught typhoid
The rain was to blame for that

Coz I'm a dirty Bertie

ENSEMBLE.
Coz he's a dirty Bertie

EDWARD VII.
Coz I am a dirty Bertie
I can't help but be a bit flirty

For sixty years I twiddled my thumbs
Waiting for Vicky to die
What did you expect me to do?
Just sit around and cry??

It all started in (*Irish accent.*) **I-re-land**
An Irish actress she
(*In RP.*) **The brigade all thought it time**
I popped my ch-her-ry

Coz I am a dirty Bertie

ENSEMBLE.
Coz he's a dirty Bertie

EDWARD VII.
Coz I am a dirty Bertie
I can't help but be a bit flirty

I was aged nineteen and without a clue
She took me by the hand
Her name was Nellie Clifden
She was anything but bland

She turned this boy into a man
She made me stand up tall

**Though I didn't last very long
Not very long at all, because...**

ENSEMBLE.
He's such a dirty Bertie

EDWARD VII.
I'm such a dirty Bertie!

ENSEMBLE.
He's such a dirty Bertie

EDWARD VII.
Loves ladies under and over thirty

(*Spoken.*) I've slept with...

This week.

**Alice, Bertha, Carol and Dee
Elsie, Fran and Gina
Hilda, Isla, Jemima, Kate
Lesley, Mags and Nina**

**Olive, Primrose, Queenie, Ruth
Susan, Tabby, Ulrika
Verity, Winnie, Xenia, Yvette
and I *think* a woman called Zena!!!**

(*Spoken – smirking.*) She was absolute filth. See I'd slipped, and before I knew it, her hand, it had gone right up my –

The ENSEMBLE *all gasp and snap into singing...*

ENSEMBLE.
He's such a dirty Bertie!

EDWARD VII (*spoken*). Oh stop it, no I'm not!

ENSEMBLE.
He's such a dirty Bertie!

EDWARD VII (*sleazily*).
Me? I'm just a little bit... flirty!

EDWARD VII *speaks the following lines. The music vamps underneath him.*

Eskimos, Red Indians, Dutch milkmaids, I've done 'em all. (*Looking quizzically at a member of the audience.*) And you, perhaps?? We haven't slept together, have we? You look a lot like your mum.

Enter COURTIER *with a telegram.*

(*Suddenly remembering.*) Oh! I've never shagged an Aborigine! Or a Geisha, or a –

COURTIER. A Senegalese Princess, your Majesty.

EDWARD VII. Yes, quite. (*Suddenly turning round to the COURTIER.*) I beg your pardon?!

The music suddenly stops.

COURTIER (*holding out the telegram*). A telegram, Your Highness, from a 'Mayor Ingram of Southend-on-Sea'.

EDWARD VII (*perplexed*). '*Southend-on-Sea*'? '*A Senegalese Princess*'? What the devil are you talking about, man?

COURTIER. Forgive me, Your Majesty, but it's with regards to an '*International Beauty Pageant*'? (*Realising their mistake.*) My apologies, I shouldn't have bothered Your Highness with such a trivial issue.

COURTIER *goes to exit.*

EDWARD VII (*stopping him*). Now, now, calm down. Let me have a read of that.

COURTIER *returns.* EDWARD VII *snatches the telegram from them and reads it.*

Tell the mayor... yes.

COURTIER (*extremely surprised*). '*Yes*'?

EDWARD VII. Did I not make myself clear?

COURTIER. Of course, Your Majesty. I shall go and inform the mayor right away.

COURTIER *makes to bow.*

EDWARD VII. Oh, and begin preparing my things – (*Looking out to the audience with a smirk.*) we're off to the seaside!

COURTIER *bows and exits.*

(*Speaking to his remaining courtiers.*) Right, you ugly lot! Time for bed! (*Smirking.*) This king needs his beauty sleep...

He bites his lip.

A blast of 'Rule Britania' plays us out as EDWARD VII *climbs back onto his sex chair and is wheeled off by his* COURTIERS. *He waves to the audience, as though he is aboard a ship.* THE BAND *and* ENSEMBLE *sing 'Rule Britainnia' with great gusto.*

ENSEMBLE.
Rule, Britannia! Britannia, rule the waves
Britons never, never, never will be slaves!

Rule, Britannia! Britannia, rule the waves
Britons never, never, never will be slaves!!!

Exit the ENSEMBLE. *The centre doors close.*

Interval.

ACT TWO

Scene One

We are outside the main entrance of the Kursaal.

Enter the BAND *who play a reprisal of 'I Do Like to Be Beside the Seaside'. This time it is more upbeat, energised.*

Present in the yard are MR ROMFORD RECORDER *and* MR DAGENHAM DAILY.

Through the stage-right door runs MR SOUTHEND STANDARD *holding a rolled-up newspaper. As he speaks, enter* NUN *through the stage-left door and who makes their way downstage.*

MR SOUTHEND STANDARD. READ ALL ABAAT IT! READ ALL ABOUT IT! SOUTHEND GOES POTTY FOR PAGEANTS!!

NUN (*addressing the audience*). You! You, all ought to be ashamed of yourselves!

> MR SOUTHEND STANDARD *and* NUN *look at one another.*

MR SOUTHEND STANDARD (*apologetically*). Sister I –

NUN (*suddenly grinning and turning back to the audience*). Just kidding! GOD, I LOVE BEAUTY PAGEANTS!!!

Cue music.

NUN *spins around in order to show off her habit.* MR SOUTHEND STANDARD *dashes over to her and the two snog. Exit* NUN *through the yard.*

MR SOUTHEND STANDARD *goes to dash after her but, spotting the centre doors opening, they jump down into the yard with the other journalists, ready for the start of press conference.*

Through the centre-stage doors enter MR BACON *and* MRS BACON, *holding hands. The two appear unified.*

MR BACON *and* MRS BACON *make their way down to downstage-centre.* MR BACON *acts as though he is the 'Big I am', waving to the audience and pointing to them as he enters.*

Having landed downstage-centre, MRS BACON *snatches her hand away from her husband's.* MR BACON *gives her a quick look, though she does not acknowledge it. He signals for the* BAND *to stop playing – they do so.*

MR BACON (*addressing the audience with great charm and enthusiasm*). Ladies and gentlemen – and I'm not just talkin' to you people of Southend, but *you*s, the peoples of the world!

How we laughed at Folkestone – I did too. But then a fought came to me, wot *is* wrong with 'celebrating womanhood'?

Here at the Kursaal, we've always liked to do fings bigger and better than anyone or anywhere else. And that ain't *no* different, when it comes to beauty pageants: *international* beauty pageants. And so this Saturday in *our* International pageant, we plan to have contestants from not only Europe –

He gestures for the crowd to give a impressed 'Wooooo' sound.

 – but, the United States of America!

He gestures for the crowd to give a impressed 'Wooooo' sound.

And yet, wot I've failed to mention is that we've one very, *very* special guest – because one of our girls will be coming all the way from Senegal –

There might or might not be a reaction from the audience.

That's in Africa.

MR SOUTHEND STANDARD, MR ROMFORD RECORDER *and* MR DAGENHAM DAILY *all gasp.*

That's right, at the Kursaal, will be the first beauty pageant in Britain's – (*Correcting himself.*) no, the *Empire's* history, to have a – (*Finding the word.*) dark woman enterin' it.

MR SOUTHEND STANDARD, MR ROMFORD RECORDER *and* MR DAGENHAM DAILY *all gasp.*

And not only that – but she's a princess!

MR SOUTHEND STANDARD, MR ROMFORD RECORDER *and* MR DAGENHAM DAILY *all gasp.*

Princess Dinubolu of Senegal.

MR SOUTHEND STANDARD, MR ROMFORD RECORDER *and* MR DAGENHAM DAILY *all begin to ask questions at the time.*

(*Interrupting.*) And so from today, *four thousand* tickets will go on sale, so you better make sure you get yours while you can!

MR ROMFORD RECORDER. *Mr Bacon! Mr Bacon!* Do you know when the princess'll be arriving?

MR BACON (*with a smirk*). She's 'ere already. She's staying with a friend.

MR ROMFORD RECORDER (*confused*). How?

MR BACON. 'How?' what?

MR ROMFORD RECORDER. *How* did she know abaat the pageant, if you've only just announced it? Don't it take a bit of time to get from Senegal?

MR BACON. Er…

MR DAGENHAM DAILY. *Mr Bacon!*

MR BACON. Yes?

MR DAGENHAM DAILY. Aren't you just a bit concerned about a repeat of the baby incident?

MR BACON *looks sheepishly* MRS BACON.

MR BACON. Well, the baby incident was a few years ago nah, and we're not talkin' abaat that, we're talking abaat the princess.

MR SOUTHEND STANDARD. 'Ow's 'aving a princess though, Mr Bacon, gonna be fair to the uvva girls?

MR BACON. What d'ya mean??

MR SOUTHEND STANDARD. Well don't you fink people will vote for the princess, *because* she's a princess and not because she's most beautiful? How's that fair on the uvvas?

MR BACON. Who said she's not beautiful?

MR SOUTHEND STANDARD. Are you saying you think she's beautiful?

MR BACON (*looking to* MRS BACON). I didn't say that.

MR ROMFORD RECORDER, MR SOUTHEND STANDARD *and* MR DAGENHAM DAILY *all begin to speak over another, asking questions.*

Thank you, gentlemen. That's all the time we have. Tickets now on sale!

MR BACON *takes* MRS BACON*'s hand and together they exit through the centre-stage doors. Eventually the* JOURNALISTS *give up and exit through the yard.*

Scene Two

It's moments after the big speech. We are round by stage door of the Kursaal.

Enter a lonely and desperate MRS BUGLE *from the yard stage-right.*

MRS BUGLE. Joanna? – JOANNA?!

MRS BUGLE *spotting stage door, makes her way over to it and knocks.*

ACT TWO, SCENE TWO 79

We hear TICKETER *unbolt the door from the inside, he opens it and greets* MRS BUGLE.

TICKETER. Hello.

MRS BUGLE. Good day, sir, excuse me, and do pardon the intrusion, but I wondered if it might be possible for me to speak to Mr Batwa on a matter of great urgency. I appear to have lost my maid – she's about – (*Gesturing.*) yay high, and she's – (*Thinking.*) got very brown hair. It suddenly dawned on me, that *he* might know where she is. And so may I speak to him, now, *please*?

TICKETER. I'm afraid you can't.

MRS BUGLE. Sir, I beg you – I wouldn't ask if it didn't mean so much.

TICKETER. You can't.

MRS BUGLE. I'll give you money, if that's what you want.

TICKETER. Money ain't gonna 'elp ya, luv, he ain't 'ere.

MRS BUGLE. Then where is he?

One of the GIRLS *comes to the door and puts her arm around* TICKETER.

ONE OF THE GIRLS (*suggestively*). *Coo-ee!*

TICKETER *turns around to see the* GIRL.

TICKETER (*a tad distracted*). Packing I reckon, last I 'eard he was leaving this week for home.

TICKETER *makes his way over to stage door to exit.*

MRS BUGLE. So he's still here?

TICKETER. Somewhere in taan I fink, but exactly where I dunno – sorry I can't be of more 'elp.

MRS BUGLE. Don't suppose you know what area of Southend / he –

The GIRL *pulls* TICKETER *in and slams the door shut.*

Enter HARRIET *from the yard, who spots* MRS BUGLE. *Following* HARRIET, *and hiding behind her fan is* VIOLET.

(*Through the door.*) We appear to have got cut off.

MRS BUGLE *waits for a moment. There is no response.*

(*Disheartened.*) Oh this is all my fault! None of this would have happened if I'd have just kept my silly, womanly, mouth shut.

MRS BUGLE *goes to shuffle off to try and find Batwa.*

HARRIET (*kindly*). Good morning, Mrs Bugle!

MRS BUGLE (*surprised to see her*). Oh, good day to you – (*Trying to remember Harriet's name.*) young / lady –

HARRIET (*pointing to herself*). / It's *Harriet* – don't worry, I work for the Bacons.

MRS BUGLE. *Harriet*, what a lovely name. How *are* Mr and Mrs Bacon? Well, I hope?

HARRIET. Yes, though very busy of course, what with news of the princess.

MRS BUGLE. What princess?

HARRIET. The one entering the beauty pageant 'ere, on Saturday. She's Senegalese.

MRS BUGLE *is quite stunned.*

MRS BUGLE. Is she? Goodness. Well would you excuse me, I must be off –

HARRIET. Yes of course.

MRS BUGLE. Do give my regards to Mr and Mrs Bacon.

MRS BUGLE *makes to exit but* HARRIET *calls after her.*

HARRIET. Er, Mrs Bugle, I 'ope – No. Don't matta. No, actually, it does. I was goin' to say that I couldn't 'elp but overhear wot you sed just nah, abaat '*Keeping your womanly, mouth shut*'?

MRS BUGLE. Oh yes?

HARRIET. And, pardon me, but I fink – I fink perhaps that it's important for yer to realise that in life, it's alright to go against the grain. That we can't control others, but we can be in control of ourselves and wot *we* do. I don't fink that 'ignorance *is* bliss'. Sometimes – (*Giving a knowing nod.*) *we* just need a little help be woken from our slumber, and so, Mrs Bugle, this an invitation from me to you to wake up, and to step out of yer ignorance and into the fire. And that all starts wiv education, and the sooner you realise that, the sooner this feeling that you're feeling, will 'av any chance of going away – D'ya understand?

A short pause as MRS BUGLE *tries to read between the lines of what* HARRIET *has just said. Slowly a thought comes to her.*

MRS BUGLE (*giving a knowing nod*). I understand entirely. Thank you, Harriet.

MRS BUGLE *exits through the yard.*

HARRIET (*waving*). Good for you, Mrs Bugle! Run! Run like the wind!

HARRIET *watches* MRS BUGLE *go, before creeping over to stage door. To her frustration she finds it locked. Suddenly* VIOLET *reveals herself from behind her fan.*

VIOLET. Good morning, Harriet!

HARRIET (*surprised*). Good morning, Violet. (*Correcting herself.*) Er, Miss Ingram.

VIOLET. I've been following you

HARRIET. Have yer? Why??

VIOLET. I've an invitation for you. I wondered if you fancied popping over some time this week? Tomorrow perhaps?

HARRIET. What for?

VIOLET. Can't girls just be friends?

A thought comes to HARRIET.

HARRIET. Will yer dad be in? Mayor Ingram?

VIOLET (*confused*). Maybe. I'll make sure there's cake.

Beat.

HARRIET (*smiling*). Why not?

VIOLET. Good. Shall we say one o'clock?

HARRIET. I'll ask Mrs Bacon if I can.

VIOLET. Good. Any problems do let me know. I'll see you then, *friend*.

Exit HARRIET *back through the yard.*

VIOLET *watches her go before exiting through the yard herself.*

Scene Three

It's the next day.

We are in the sitting room of Batwa's house. BATWA *and* JOANNA *are in but elsewhere. Enter an annoyed* MRS BACON *through the stage-left door, followed by* MR BACON.

MR BACON. Luv, please!

MRS BACON. I just don't know who she is, Parsley! Or where she's come from, what she knows abaat me, you, *us*?

MR BACON. She doesn't know anyfing abaat us, luv. It's simply a business arrangement.

MRS BACON. Have you forgotten everyfing that happened wiv that Negro baby?

MR BACON. Course I ain't.

MRS BACON. I told you to hold a baby competition –

MR BACON. And I did.

MRS BACON. – what I did *not* tell you to do was to put a Black baby in it, only for said baby to go and win.

MR BACON (*nonchalant*). It was different, people like different, sometimes.

MRS BACON. For weeks afterwards we woz *mobbed*, whenever we went aat –

MR BACON *and* MRS BACON *speak at the same time:*

| MRS BACON. '*Why couldn't you give the prize to a baby of your own colour?*', '*What do you mean by this?*', '*How could you dare?*' | MR BACON. I know! I was there. What can I say? I heard 'em. I nearly lost me job! Controversy sells. |

MRS BACON. The shame that baby bought not only to us, but the entire taan –

MR BACON. It weren't the baby's fault, luv.

MRS BACON. I know that, I'm not saying it woz.

MR BACON. But didn't I fix it? Didn't I? *I* got the Kursaal to fix all that; nah all anyone eva finks abaat when they fink about Southend ain't that baby, but the building; the lights, the arcades.

MRS BACON. Well, let's hope it stays that way.

MR BACON. It will, trust me.

Beat.

MRS BACON. Do you fink she's beautiful?

MR BACON. Who?

MRS BACON *just stares at her husband.*

I only 'av eyes for you.

Enter JOANNA, *in a dressing gown. She has her undergarments on underneath though we do not see this at this time. An anxious* BATWA *follows her.*

BATWA. Joanna, please, I'm begging you –

Spotting MR BACON *and* MRS BACON, *he stops.*

MRS BACON. Did you find anything useful up there, Mr Batwa?

BATWA (*hesitantly*). I think so. I've left it in the attic, laid out.

MRS BACON. Lovely. Right, let's go take a look.

> MRS BACON *exits through the stage-right door followed by* MR BACON.

BATWA (*pleading*). Joanna –

JOANNA. Mr Batwa, perhaps you should ask yourself, 'ow any of what I'm abaat to do is any different to what you do?

BATWA. Of course it's different. It's completely different, mine is a *performance*.

JOANNA. So is this.

BATWA. Mine is not a lie. I am a pygmy and proud to be so.

JOANNA. You forget, sir, that I *am* part African myself, 'a half-caste', as you so mentioned the other day, and proud to be so. Africa is just as much in my blood, as it is alive in yours.

BATWA. But you don't know what you're doing!

JOANNA. I do.

BATWA. So what *exactly do* '*Royals*' do then??

> JOANNA *struggles to find the words, in truth, she isn't quite sure.*

JOANNA. 'Servitude.' Just of a different kind.

BATWA. And just who is it you're 'serving'? Because it certainly isn't the people of Senegal, because they have no idea you exist!

JOANNA (*cocky*). They'll never find aat.

BATWA. That you're a con artist?

Beat.

JOANNA *is wounded.*

JOANNA. Nah, that's a very dangerous word to be throwing abaat, Mr Batwa.

BATWA. But it's *true*.

JOANNA. The people will only see what I want 'em to see, Mr Batwa.

BATWA. But, Joanna, you can't win! *The crown*. It isn't a good thing.

JOANNA. D'ya know wot? I'm beginning to regret ever 'aving met yer.

BATWA and JOANNA are wounded.

Enter MRS BACON through the stage-right door, followed by MR BACON, who carries a selection of clothing.

MRS BACON. My goodness, Mr Batwa, such a treasure trove up there. Haven't you got abaat?

BATWA. The colonel is a great collector.

MRS BACON instructs MR BACON to place it on the floor.

MRS BACON. (*to* JOANNA). Nah, we couldn't bring it all daan of course, so just brought the bits we need. (*Implying* BATWA *and* MR BACON *should leave*.) Gentlemen.

MR BACON and BATWA do as they are told and leave the room.

Right, Princess, let's get you ready. (*Referring to the dressing gown*.) Drop it. And put these on.

JOANNA does as she is told, and takes off her dressing gown. Throughout the following dialogue, MRS BACON hands African attire and accessories to JOANNA. JOANNA puts them on.

JOANNA. Is sunink wrong, Mrs Bacon?

MRS BACON (*firmly*). No, luv.

JOANNA. Are you sure?

Beat.

MRS BACON. We were just talking abaat that baby that won a few years back.

JOANNA. Yes, I've been finking abaat that baby too, and 'ow if it won, this should be an easy win for me as well.

MRS BACON (*sarcastically*). Should it? You eva played an African princess before then?

JOANNA. No.

MRS BACON. So there is a chance then that this could all go very wrong and you could take us all wiv yer?

JOANNA. All I want is to enter a beauty pageant.

MRS BACON. Yes, but *why*??

JOANNA goes to speak but can't find the words.

(*Calling out for* MR BACON *and* BATWA.) BOYS!

I like the name by the way, 'Dinubolu', how'dya just come up wiv that?

JOANNA (*shrugs*). I just fought it sounded '*African-y*'.

MRS BACON. Very good.

Enter a rather excited MR BACON, *followed by* BATWA, *who stands looking at* JOANNA.

MR BACON circles JOANNA *and, after a while of taking in her new look, gives a look of uncertainty to* MRS BACON.

MRS BACON. Well??

MR BACON. I don't know, luv. I fink she looks *too African*, you know?

JOANNA. But that's what I am, an African princess –

BATWA. Senegalese.

MRS BACON. Yeah, that one.

JOANNA (*enjoying the feel of the material on her skin*). I like it.

ACT TWO, SCENE THREE 37

MR BACON. I just worry, luv, it's a bit *too* much, that's all –

A sudden knock on the front door. ALL *look at each other in a panic.*

No one panic, it's probably just the press.

There's another knock.

MRS BACON. Bloody vultures.

There's another knock. It then continues.

MRS BUGLE (*speaking slowing through the door*). Mr Batwa. Excuse me. I'm Mrs Bugle.

JOANNA. Oh fudge.

MRS BUGLE (*continuing to speak patronisingly through the door*). Can I have a minute of your time and then, I promise, I shan't bother you again.

MR BACON (*perplexed*). What the 'ell is she doing 'ere?

JOANNA. I fink she's here for me? I work for 'er. (*Correcting herself.*) Well I did – she's me mistress.

MRS BACON (*greatly concerned*). Are you a local? Does that mean people in this taan might recognise yer? (*Turning her head to glare at* MR BACON.) Did you know that??

MR BACON. Luv, please.

MRS BUGLE (*from the other side of the door*). Mr Batwa??

MR BACON (*to* BATWA). Don't open it, she'll soon get the hint.

BATWA. This is my house. I shall do what I like.

BATWA *makes straight for the door. In the process,* MR BACON *and* MRS BACON *dart down towards the stage-right pillar and casually lean on it, while* JOANNA *hides behind the other pillar on stage-left.*

BATWA *opens the door. We see* MR SOUTHEND STANDARD, MR ROMFORD RECORD *and* MR

DAGENHAM DAILY *baying at the door. Enter a rather flustered* MRS BUGLE *dressed in an African kaftan and large beads.*

MRS BUGLE (*speaking to the journalists*). Get away, you! Shoo! Shoo! Shoo! –

Upon entering and the door closing behind her, MRS BUGLE *spots the* BACONS.

Oh Mr and Mrs Bacon!? I wasn't expecting you here?

MR BACON *and* MRS BACON *anxiously look at one another.*

MRS BACON. Likewise.

BATWA. Was there something that you wanted, Mrs Bugle?

Surprised by his excellent English, MRS BUGLE *stares at* BATWA *for just a moment before speaking.*

MRS BUGLE. Er, yes, quite. (*Gathering her thoughts.*) You see, my maid; my housekeeper –

BATWA. Does she have a name??

MRS BUGLE. *Joanna.* Her name is – was – Joanna. See, she left us – me, after a 'little spatter'. Things suddenly got so terribly out of hand, and before I knew it, she'd gathered her things, and left.

BATWA (*aware there was a reason*). Do you know why?

MRS BUGLE. Not really.

BATWA. There must have been a reason.

MRS BUGLE. Well, the night before, we'd been to see you in your little show – (*Correcting herself.*) – *show*, at (*Gesturing to* MR BACON.) the Kursaal.

BATWA. And?? What happened?

MRS BUGLE. Well, the next day we were talking about it – *you* specifically – and she – Joanna– said she felt sorry for you; said she didn't like the way you were being treated, in front of so many – that you have feelings.

ACT TWO, SCENE THREE

BATWA. –

MRS BUGLE. I tried to tell her she was being ridiculous, tried to explain that someone like you doesn't feel the way we feel, understand like we do, but she wouldn't listen, and well, the last thing she said to me, was that she was going to find you, to try and save you from the likes of us.

BATWA. –

MRS BUGLE. I thought that you might have run away together – though clearly not as you're still here – but I wonder, is she here too?? Joanna? Because if she is, I'd very much like to tell her how sorry I am and that I'd like for her to come back, because home isn't quite the same without her, and if I am being honest with myself, as one really should – I miss her.

Silence.

(*An afterthought.*) Oh, and then she said something about a beauty pageant.

Beat.

BATWA. Mrs Bugle –

MRS BUGLE (*apologetically*). I'm educated, now – I went to London: the Exhibition Centre, turns out there's a delightful exhibit: a Senegalese village. Though it's not a real village of course, fake you understand but with real mud huts and villagers, around a hundred or so; men, women and children. All quite spectacular. And all to celebrate His Majesty's Entente Cordiale. I must assure you and your people that, when once ignorance was bliss, it is quite frankly no more.

Silence.

BATWA *is wounded.*

BATWA. I'm afraid, Mrs Bugle, Joanna isn't / here –

JOANNA, *now transformed into* PRINCESS DINUBOLU, *emerges from behind the pillar; her sudden appearance makes* MRS BUGLE *jump.*

MRS BUGLE. Oh good heavens! Who are you?

PRINCESS DINUBOLU (*mimicking Mrs Bugle's RP accent and enjoying the sounds*). Who are you?

MRS BUGLE (*confused*). I'm Mrs Bugle.

JOANNA. Mrs Bugle.

MRS BUGLE. Yes I am, who are you?

PRINCESS DINUBOLU (*proudly*). *I* – am *Princess Dinubolu of Senegal.*

MRS BUGLE. Good heavens! (*She bows.*) Forgive me, Your Majesty. I wasn't aware of your being here.

PRINCESS DINUBOLU. Yes, so it would seem.

MRS BUGLE. My sincerest apologies, your Majesty for any –

PRINCESS DINUBOLU. Your sorries – they mean absolutely nothing to me. You came for your maid. She is not here. Perhaps, then, you should leave?

MRS BUGLE. (*Apologetically*) Yes, yes, I… Of course.

A moment as MRS BUGLE *stares at* PRINCESS DINUBOLU *– there is something familiar about her.*

Thank you, Your Majesty.

MRS BUGLE *curtsies, and begins walking backwards until she reaches the front door.* MR BACON *then opens the door – we see* MR SOUTHEND STANDARD, MR ROMFORD RECORDER *and* MR DAGENHAM DAILY *– they harass* MRS BUGLE *as she exits.* MR BACON *slams the door shut.*

JOANNA, MR BACON *and* MRS BACON *all look at one another.*

Beat. Beat. Beat.

The three then begin to scream with excitement; they run towards each other and congratulate each other. Unseen by the others, BATWA *makes his way over to the front door.*

JOANNA. Did ya see that?! Did ya see me?! It was like there woz this voice in me 'art, and it was like *'Don't do it Joanna! Don't do it!'*, but then suddenly me 'ead woz like, 'DO IT NOW! DO IT NOW!!'

MRS BACON. 'Ere, do that again!

JOANNA. Alright – (*Pretending to be Princess Dinubolu again.*) '*Your sorries – they mean absolutely nothing to me.*'

JOANNA, MRS BACON *and* MR BACON *all burst out laughing.*

MR BACON (*tapping* MRS BACON *on the arm*). Ere, luv –

MR BACON *calmly walks over to* JOANNA.

Your Majesty.

MR BACON *bows and goes to take* JOANNA*'s hand but before he can –*

We hear two very controlled knocks. It's COUSIN ARTHUR.

JOANNA, MR BACON *and* MRS BACON *look to the door. They find* BATWA *standing right by it.*

We hear the same two knocks again.

BATWA *makes the decision to step away from the door.*

COUSIN ARTHUR (*on the other side of the door*). Knock knock.

MR BACON (*shouting towards the door*). Who's there?

Beat.

COUSIN ARTHUR (*through the door*). Postman.

Beat.

I've got post.

MR BACON. Hang abaat – Arfur?!

Beat.

COUSIN ARTHUR (*through the door*). Yeh.

MR BACON *quickly opens the door. Enter* COUSIN ARTHUR *with a telegram in hand. We see the* JOURNALISTS *as the door is opened and shut.*

COUSIN ARTHUR (*unenthusiastically*). Alright, Parsley? (*To* MRS BACON.) Jessie? –

He holds out the telegram for someone to take.

Telegram.

BATWA *walks over to* COUSIN ARTHUR *and goes to take it.*

COUSIN ARTHUR *brings the telegram nearer to his chest.*

COUSIN ARTHUR. Sorry sir, ain't for you. It's for a '*Princess Dinubolu*' (*He looks over at* JOANNA.) That you?

JOANNA. Yeh.

COUSIN ARTHUR (*handing her the letter*). 'Ere you go then Your Majesty. Have a good day.

Turning to MR BACON *and* MRS BACON.

See ya.

COUSIN ARTHUR *exits.* JOANNA *stands staring at the telegram.*

MRS BACON. Well, what is it?

JOANNA. I don't know.

MR BACON. Well, open it.

JOANNA. I don't want to.

MR BACON. Why?!

JOANNA (*showing the royal seal*). Coz it looks important.

MRS BACON. Oh for goodness' sake! Gives it 'ere.

MRS BACON *quickly takes the telegram and reads it. She then holds the letter close to her chest and looks up to God. She's worried.*

BATWA. What is it? What's wrong?!

MR BACON (*worried*). Who's it from, luv?

Beat.

Who's it from, luv?

MRS BACON (*shocked*). The King.

BATWA. '*The King*'?! What does he want?

MRS BACON. It's an invitation –

MR BACON. To wot??

MRS BACON. To meet 'im.

JOANNA *excitedly looks towards* BATWA.

JOANNA. At Buckingham Palace?!

MRS BACON. No – not at Buckingham Palace.

Beat.

He's coming 'ere – to Southend.

All four stand, stunned.

BATWA. Joanna, you can't. The crown –

JOANNA. Mr Batwa, I cannot say no to the King, that would be rude, and one cannot be rude to the King. (*Cocky.*) Besides we *'av* time.

MRS BACON. No we ain't.

JOANNA. Why?! When's 'e coming?

MRS BACON. Friday.

JOANNA. But that's in free days' time?

MRS BACON (*concerned*). And he'll be staying for the pageant – apparently. He wishes yer the best of luck.

JOANNA. I ain't eva met a king before, I wonder what 'e's like, *Edward*?

BATWA (*anxiously*). Joanna –

JOANNA. Where am I to meet 'im exactly? The Kursaal?

MR BACON *takes the telegram from* MRS BACON *and reads.*

MR BACON. Says 'ere, the 'Palace Hotel', on the front. He's inviting yer '...*to discuss matters of a diplomatic nature*'.

BATWA (*worried*). Joanna – it's not too late, you know –

MRS BACON. Parsley, we need to 'ead back for you to give Harriet some money, and me to tell 'er what to pick up from the 'aberdashery.

(*Pointing to* BATWA.) You – keep an eye on 'er. We'll be back tomorra.

MR BACON *opens the door for* MRS BACON *to exit through – she does so. He too then leaves, with the last we see of him being him being harassed by the* JOURNALISTS *outside.* JOANNA *and* BATWA *are left alone.* JOANNA *makes to exit stage-right.*

BATWA (*matter-of-fact*). You know they speak French in Senegal.

JOANNA *freezes, and tries her best to suppress her panic.*

JOANNA. Don't matter. Everyone speaks English anyway.

JOANNA *exits stage-right. We have a moment with* BATWA *alone onstage by himself – he has an air of sadness about him. He too then exits stage-right.*

Scene Four

We're at the Ingram's house.

Enter HARRIET *and* VIOLET *from stage-left. Both are reading beauty magazines.*

A thought comes to HARRIET.

HARRIET. You know, some say make-up is an extension of the patriarch, and that women wear it not for themselves, as they like to claim, but to entertain the male gaze; an unrealistic ideology placed on them by men, who themselves make no attempt to abide by the same unattainable standards.

VIOLET (*smiling*). Goodness, aren't you jolly? You know so much.

HARRIET. Not really, I reckon you know just as much as me, it's just that I've started asking more questions of late.

VIOLET. How thrilling.

HARRIET. See, people try to tell us that we're from different sides of the track. But what track? Coz I can't see no track. So what is it that's keeping us a part? Or should that be *who*? And why are they so afraid of *us* talking?

VIOLET (*concerned*). Why?

HARRIET. Because they're afraid of the likes of you and me questioning the status quo, because if we question it, that means we see it, and if we see it, it means we see them.

VIOLET (*worried*). Who?

HARRIET goes take out her suffragette newsletter from her pocket to show to VIOLET but, before she can, MAYOR INGRAM interrupts.

MAYOR INGRAM (*shouting offstage*). Violet! Violet, darling!? Daddy's home! Are you in?

VIOLET rolls her eyes, and stands to greet her father.

VIOLET (*snippy*). Yeh, and I've company.

Enter MAYOR INGRAM through the stage-left door, being closely followed by BERNARD. Upon entering, MAYOR INGRAM makes his way over to VIOLET and kisses her on the head.

MAYOR INGRAM (*addressing* VIOLET). Hello dearest!

HARRIET. Afternoon Mayor Ingram!

MAYOR INGRAM. Oh. Violet didn't mention she had a friend over.

VIOLET. Daddy, can you leave us please?

MAYOR INGRAM. Of course. In that case, would you both excuse us, times are busy what with the princess *and* His Majesty coming –

VIOLET (*sarcastically*). Yes, we know, you've barely mentioned it.

MAYOR INGRAM. A third re-election depends on it. Something never done before. But let us not get too ahead of ourselves – (*Excitedly.*) I'm testing my welcome speech on Bernard, here.

BERNARD *nods*.

VIOLET. Well go and do it then.

MAYOR INGRAM. Yes, very good dear, very good – '*Time waits for no man.*'

As MAYOR INGRAM *and* BERNARD *go to exit through the stage-right door,* HARRIET *suddenly calls out.*

HARRIET. MAYOR INGRAM! YOU KNOW THE PAGEANT ON SATURDAY? CAN YOU 'AVE A WORD WITH MR BACON ABAAT LETTING ME ENTA IT?! – PLEASE!

A brief moment of awkwardness.

MAYOR INGRAM (*patronisingly*). My dear – one can hardly imagine Mr or Mrs Bacon would want their maid participating in a beauty pageant – it just isn't the done thing. And besides, only one girl can represent their country, and it's Violet who's representing England – Bernard, let's to my study?

Exit MAYOR INGRAM *and* BERNARD. HARRIET *and* VIOLET *watch them go. As soon as they are gone, a disappointed* HARRIET *makes to leave.*

VIOLET. Wait! Where are you going?

HARRIET (*disappointed*). Home.

VIOLET. Home? But why? Wait! I need you. I can't do this without you. (*A thought comes to her.*) Wait! What if you came with me, backstage?

HARRIET. 'Backstage'?

VIOLET. Be my dresser; My lady-in-waiting, my confidante. If you aren't allowed *on*stage, perhaps the next best thing is *backstage* with me?

HARRIET. Is that why you invited me over?

VIOLET. Not exactly. I must confess that my real reason for my inviting you over is, I figured, since you are working for the Bacons, you must have all the inside gossip; gossip that might help me win. Particularly now I so find myself up against, of all people, an African princess.

HARRIET. But you're beautiful.

VIOLET. No I'm not.

HARRIET (*sincerely*). Yes you are, course you are. Look at yer! – Okay, I'll 'elp yer.

VIOLET. You will?

HARRIET. Yes.

VIOLET. Really??

HARRIET. Yes.

VIOLET *squeals*.

(*Eagerly.*) Right, come on then – wot's the first fing you wanna know?

VIOLET. Okay, what have the Bacons said the competition will entail, exactly?

HARRIET. Er, well, I fink they said sunink abaat the girls havin' to walk up and down –

VIOLET. Good –

HARRIET. And dance a bit.

VIOLET. '*Dance*'?! But I can't *dance*!

HARRIET. Gonna be taught one on the day, apparently. (*Thinking*.) What woz that funny word they kept using? – '*Formations*'.

VIOLET. '*Formations*'? What on earth are they?

HARRIET. Oh! And they said sunink abaat 'ow you girls would do good to '*Bring yourselves to the pageant*'.

VIOLET. '*Bring ourselves to the pageant*'?! What does that mean?! I am bringing myself! How can I be there, if I don't bring myself?

HARRIET. I dunno.

VIOLET. This is gonna be a complete disaster! You just know, those girls are all gonna rock up –

VIOLET *and* HARRIET. And all *glare* at each other.

HARRIET. Well then, it's a good fing I'll be there now to glare back at 'em wiv yer.

VIOLET. Oh Harriet. Thank you. Together we can't lose.

HARRIET. No, we can't.

VIOLET. For England?

HARRIET *and* VIOLET. FOR ENGLAND!!

Exit VIOLET *and* HARRIET *through the stage-left door.*

Scene Five

It's Friday. The day before the pageant.

Moving to the front of Juliet's balcony, the BAND *come together to play a royal-trumpety piece of music. We are now outside the Palace Hotel, the finest hotel Southend has to offer.*

ACT TWO, SCENE FIVE 99

The centre doors open. Enter VIOLET *who holds a little Union Jack flag in one hand and a French flag in the other. Enter* REGINALD *and* BERNARD *who roll out the red carpet from the centre-stage doors.*

Enter then MR BACON *and* MRS BACON, *who also carry a little Union Jack flag and a French flag. All form a line and wait.*

MR BACON. You've done a great job, luv.

MRS BACON. God 'elp us if that gell gets found aat.

MR BACON. She won't.

MRS BACON. You better be sure abaat dat.

As the music builds, suddenly MAYOR INGRAM (*with his civic regalia*) *dashes in. He gestures to all that 'She's coming!', and cues the* BAND *to enthusiastically begin playing the French national anthem ('La Marseillaise').*

As the song plays, those onstage try their best to sing along. ALL *wave their little flags.*

Enter a very confident and composed PRINCESS DINUBOLU. *She is dressed in a red dress – Western in style. She lands downstage-centre.*

ALL.
Allons enfants de la Patrie
Le jour de gloire est arrivé!
Contre nous de la tyrannie
L'étendard sanglant est levé
L'étendard sanglant est levé
Entendez-vous dans les campagnes
Mugir ces féroces soldats?
Ils viennent jusque dans vos bras
Égorger nos fils, nos compagnes!

Aux armes, citoyens
Formez vos bataillons
Marchons, marchons!
Qu'un sang impur
Abreuve nos sillons!

Step forward MAYOR INGRAM, *who bows to* PRINCESS DINUBOLU, *before gesturing to* VIOLET *to quickly come over. She does so, awkwardly curtsies, and steps back.*

MAYOR INGRAM. Your Highness. On behalf of the people of Southend-on-Sea – (*Gesturing to audience.*) I, Mayor Ingram, would like to welcome you, to our town.

PRINCESS DINUBOLU (*in RP*). The pleasure is all mine, Mayor, Southend's reputation precedes itself.

MAYOR INGRAM. Your Highness, you are too kind. If I may, I would like to invite you to kindly utter a few words to *us*, your newest and most loyal of subjects, on that what you will.

A concerned PRINCESS DINBOLU *looks to* MR BACON *and* MRS BACON. *Having no choice but to step forward, she does so and thinks of what to say. Several times she attempts to utter something, but nothing comes out.*

(*Encouragingly.*) Perhaps Her Majesty, might like to explain her reasoning for coming here; for entering the pageant?

PRINCESS DINUBOLU. Yes, very good. (*She gathers herself.*) I am here –

PRINCESS DINUBOLU *looks around for inspiration and in the process spots* THE BAND *up on the balcony.*

– because of love.

MAYOR INGRAM. '*Love*'??

MR BACON *and* MRS BACON *look at one another.*

PRINCESS DINUBOLU (*almost surprising herself*). Yes. I am in love. Deeply.

MAYOR INGRAM. With who?!

PRINCESS DINUBOLU. A musician.

MR BACON. Your Maj/esty –

PRINCESS DINUBOLU *begins get carried away in the moment.* MR BACON *and* MRS BACON *look on helplessly.*

ACT TWO, SCENE FIVE   101

PRINCESS DINUBOLU. / We fled Africa. My lover and I – together. Arm in arm. His name – was *Tomtom*.

MAYOR INGRAM. Was?

PRINCESS DINUBOLU. – *is*. And he too, like me – of course – is from Senegal; a land where the plains glisten in the sun, where the rivers run clear, and nature plays its sweet song both day and night.

I told him of our love.

MAYOR INGRAM. Who??

PRINCESS DINUBOLU. My Father – the Chief, of Senegal.

'Marry a musician?!', he boomed. *'That's not a real job! The shame it will bring to our family. I don't care that you love him. A princess simply cannot.'*

Tomtom and I tried everything to persuade him, but alack, he was having none of it.

And so torn between the love of my father and the love of my life, I soon came to realise that the only way 'Papa' might relent was if I was to enter an international beauty pageant, and win, but not just any international beauty pageant, an international beauty pageant that takes place in the entertainment capital of the world.

MAYOR INGRAM. But, why?

PRINCESS DINUBOLU. You've questions – lots, I'm sure – but forgive me, as my English is a little, how you say, '*not so good*'.

MAYOR INGRAM. Your Majesty, thank you. I, *we*, then, wish you the best of luck in your endeavour, to be crowned *Miss Southend 1908* in tomorrow's beauty pageant, down at the Kursaal.

VIOLET, BERNARD, REGINALD, MR BACON *and* MRS BACON *all clap*.

Suddenly, from the balcony, MUSICIAN *spots* EDWARD VII *and* COURTIER *approaching through the yard*.

MUSICIAN. IT'S THE KING!

The BAND *immediately begin to play the British national anthem, 'God Save the King'.* BERNARD *and* REGINALD *each head to a downstage corner and encourage the audience to sing along.*

ALL *except* EDWARD VII *sing the British National Anthem.*

ALL.
God save our gracious King
Long live our noble King
God save the King!
Send him victorious
Happy and glorious
Long to reign over us…
God save the King!

Once onstage, EDWARD VII *stands downstage-centre with* COURTIER *standing apart from him.* PRINCESS DINUBOLU *and* EDWARD VII *stand facing each other. The two royals begin to engage in a game of weird, awkward flirting.*

EDWARD VII (*smug, but genuine*). God, I love that song.

Beat.

Princess Dinubolu, I presume?

PRINCESS DINUBOLU. That is me.

EDWARD VII. 'Princess of Senegal', eh?

PRINCESS DINUBOLU. Indeed.

EDWARD VII. Beautiful country.

PRINCESS DINUBOLU (*with a touch of panic in her voice*). Have you been?!

EDWARD VII. No.

PRINCESS DINUBOLU. Good.

EDWARD VII. But I've always thought the French to have excellent taste.

PRINCESS DINUBOLU. Indeed they do, / Your Majesty –

EDWARD VII. / La Coeur a ses raisons que la raison ne connait point. [The heart has its reasons of which reason knows nothing.]

Having absolutely no idea what EDWARD VII *has just said,* PRINCESS DINUBOLU *simply stares at him.* EDWARD VII *waits for a response. The two hold each other's gaze.*

In a bid to break the awkwardness, MAYOR INGRAM *politely interrupts. He addresses* EDWARD VII. EDWARD VII *and* PRINCESS DINUBOLU *continue to make eye contact.*

MAYOR INGRAM. Your Majesty. On behalf of the people of Southend-on-Sea – (*Gesturing to audience.*) I, Mayor Ingram, would like to welcome you to our / town –

EDWARD VII (*glancing behind him at the Palace Hotel*). / Is this it then??

MAYOR INGRAM. What?

EDWARD VII (*disdainfully*). '*The Palace Hotel.*' Doesn't look anything like a palace.

MAYOR INGRAM. I assure you, Your Majesty, it's the best hotel Southend has to offer.

EDWARD VII *looks to* COURTIER *to check if that's true;* COURTIER *nods.*

EDWARD VII (*to* PRINCESS DINUBOLU). Very well in that case, shall we?

He offers his hand to her for her to rest her hand upon.

Your Majesty...

EDWARD VII *holds his hand out for* JOANNA *to take. Having no idea of how to respond to such a gesture,* JOANNA *looks over to* MR BACON *and* MRS BACON *for help. They very subtly try their best to give her a clue as to what to do. Believing herself to have understood,* PRINCESS DINUBOLU *slowly walks over to* EDWARD VII, *and slaps her hand in his.*

MAYOR INGRAM *then leads* PRINCESS DINUBOLU, EDWARD VII *and* COURTIER *around the stage and back to centre. Exit* VIOLET, BERNARD *and* REGINALD *stage-left. A concerned* MR BACON *and* MRS BACON *look at one other, worried, before too exiting stage-left.*

Scene Six

We are now in the best suite at the Palace Hotel.

A chaise longue is wheeled on through the centre-stage doors, as is a tray on which we see a decanter of whisky, along with two tumbler glasses, and a fruit platter consisting of grapes, oranges, apples and pineapples.

MAYOR INGRAM. Here we – are...!

MAYOR INGRAM *walks to the front of the stage.*

The best view, in the whole of Essex! From here you can see the pier – the world's longest – the Kursaal, of course, and to the right – (*Proudly.*) you'll note a statue of the late, great, Queen Victor/ia

EDWARD VII (*brat-like*). / YES, THANK YOU VERY MUCH! That will be all!

COURTIER *opens one of the centre-stage doors.* MAYOR INGRAM *has outstayed his welcome.*

MAYOR INGRAM. Yes of course. Have a good evening, Your Majesties.

MAYOR INGRAM *bows and exits through the doors. He is then followed by* COURTIER.

COURTIER (*whilst closing the door*). Your Majesty.

EDWARD VII *makes his way over to the tray.*

EDWARD VII. Would you like a drink?

JOANNA *stands in awe of the King.*

ACT TWO, SCENE SIX

(*Smiling.*) I assure you, it isn't a difficult question. Would you like a drink?

JOANNA. Yes please.

EDWARD VII. Good, I was hoping you'd say that.

He pours them both a glass.

You'll like it, I assure you. It's one of my own, in fact, I make it myself – (*Correcting himself.*) well not me, but you know –

EDWARD VII *hands to* JOANNA *her glass.*

Here.

He then raises his own.

Cheers.

The two clink glasses. EDWARD VII *downs his drink and so walks over to the trolley to pour another.* JOANNA *takes a sip of hers, and though she coughs, she thoroughly enjoys it, and so downs most of it.*

'*Princess Dinubolu*' – am I saying that right? (*Saying it a tad slower, so as to enjoy the sounds.*) '*Princess Dinubolu of Senegal*' – Is that it??

PRINCESS DINUBOLU. What do you mean?

EDWARD VII. Well, I mean – ask me *my* full title.

PRINCESS DINUBOLU. Very well. 'What is your full title?'

EDWARD VII (*pointing to her*). Good question. (*Announcing it.*)'*King Edward VII: King of the United Kingdom of Great Britain and Ireland, and of the British Dominions Beyond the Seas, Defender of the Faith, Emperor of India.*'

– Quite the mouthful, don't you think?

PRINCESS DINUBOLU. Yes, quite.

EDWARD VII (*with sincerity*). How do you feel about it? (*Pointing to her glass.*) Top-up??

He doesn't wait for her answer but goes and gets the bottle to do so anyway.

How does hearing that make you feel?

PRINCESS DINUBOLU *thinks*.

PRINCESS DINUBOLU (*genuinely*). Proud.

EDWARD VII. 'Proud'? Even though you're African? Even though you represent the French? Hearing what I just said makes you 'proud'?

JOANNA *thinks while* EDWARD VII *tops up her drink*.

PRINCESS DINUBOLU. No actually, I don't think it does.

EDWARD VII. 'No'? Goodness, my lady, are you always so quick to change your mind?

PRINCESS DINUBOLU. No.

EDWARD VII (*teasingly*). No? – Yes, no, maybe so.

EDWARD VII *smirks, walks over to the tray, returns the decanter and samples some grapes.*

PRINCESS DINUBOLU. I say 'no' because – well I wonder why – and forgive me Your Majesty – why one man, one country perhaps, needs so much.

EDWARD VII (*with his mouth full*). Ahh! Now we're getting somewhere.

EDWARD VII *gestures for* PRINCESS DINUBOLU *to sit next to him on the chaise longue. He sits.* PRINCESS DINUBOLU *remains where she is.*

Oh come now, if there stands any chance at all of our two great nations developing some sort of relationship, it should probably start with us.

PRINCESS DINUBOLU *makes her way over to the chaise longue and sits.* EDWARD VII *combs her hair behind her ear.*

Shall I tell you a little secret?

Sometimes – Lord, if Mother could hear me now, she'd be utterly ashamed – but sometimes I too wonder the very same thing: 'Is it *fair*?' But then, as quick as the thought's there, it's gone.

'Tis a funny old thing, this Empire business, being in charge of a quarter of the world's population I assure you certainly doesn't come without its challenges.

For a long time I doubted I was ever up to it, blasphemous I know, considering the crown is a divine right – and I have to admit that I've always thought it rather peculiar that in those moments of doubt, God himself never came to me, as being the Defender of Faith, the man practically has a direct line.

Anyway, one day– as if by magic or miracle – it dawned on me, that perhaps I was asking the wrong question. Not, 'Why am I worthy of the crown and everything that comes with it?' but 'Why *shouldn't I* be worthy of it and all that it brings?', and just like that – (*He clicks his fingers.*) everything clicked into place: that I, as King, a man blessed with the honour, the *responsibility*, of wearing a crown, have no need to justify my myself to any person – myself included – simply because of the hat that rests on my head.

Though I'm not wearing it now, of course, it's far too bloody heavy, but you get the point.

Beat.

Tell me, what *is* it like in Senegal? What will you show me?

PRINCESS DINUBOLU *appears frightened. She fears this is the moment she must confess who she really is.*

PRINCESS DINUBOLU. Your Majesty, I fear / I must –

EDWARD VII. / Fear not, old gal, us Brits shan't be taking over Senegal anytime soon, that belongs to the French – neither have we any intent for that matter to conquer Somalia or the Congo –

PRINCESS DINUBOLU. The Congo??

EDWARD VII. Goodness, yes, I might be rich and powerful but I'm not mad. The Belgians can keep that. King Leopold's nothing but a genocidal maniac. The stories coming out for that country are nothing less than horrific: mutilation, starvation, raids, enslavement of men, women – and children, interestingly enough.

PRINCESS DINUBOLU *stands up*.

Is something wrong?

PRINCESS DINUBOLU. Would you excuse me, Your Majesty, I must go.

EDWARD VII. Why?? Have I've frightened you old gal? If so, I apologise entirely, it certainly was not my intent. (*Taking her hand.*) Now, why don't you sit down, calm your nerves?

PRINCESS DINUBOLU. I mustn't.

EDWARD VII (*patronisingly*). *Your Highness*, remember who you're talking to.

PRINCESS DINUBOLU *sits*. EDWARD VII *lifts her drink to her lips and tips the glass so she drinks, every last drop.*

There. Better?

PRINCESS DINUBOLU *nods,* EDWARD VII *then suddenly kisses her.*

PRINCESS DINUBOLU/JOANNA *is wounded*.

Forgive me, old gal, I couldn't resist.

EDWARD VII *goes to kiss her again, this time* PRINCESS DINUBOLU *stands up. As* EDWARD VII *goes to take her hand,* PRINCESS DINUBOLU *snatches it away.*

PRINCESS DINUBOLU. I said I must go, and I meant it. I shall see you tomorrow at the pageant, Your Majesty.

PRINCESS DINUBOLU *makes to leave*.

EDWARD VII. What makes you think you can win that thing, eh? Because you can't.

ACT TWO, SCENE SIX   109

May I remind you that much of the way the world thinks, speaks and sees is through my eyes, and right now, all I see is nothing more than a pathetic novelty.

PRINCESS DINUBOLU/JOANNA *is wounded again. She runs off.*

As she opens the centre-stage doors to exit, MR BACON, MRS BACON *and* MAYOR INGRAM *all fall through the doors.* JOANNA *runs past and over them.* MR BACON *quickly gets up, and goes to help his wife.*

MRS BACON. Get after 'er! I'll catch you up.

MR BACON *does as he is told and runs after* JOANNA. MRS BACON *and* MAYOR INGRAM *both get up, only to find themselves standing in front of* EDWARD VII.

MAYOR INGRAM (*tentatively*). Your Majesty, on behalf of myself and the council, I sincerely hope that what has happened here tonight does not make you feel the need to leave before tomorrow's proceedings –

EDWARD VII. FRANZ!

Enter COURTIER, *who looks around the room, only to notice the princess gone.*

COURTIER. Your Majesty?

COURTIER *looks to* EDWARD VII.

EDWARD VII. We're leaving.

EDWARD VII, *followed by* COURTIER, *storms over to the door.*

MAYOR INGRAM. Your Majesty, please.

MRS BACON *curtsies to* EDWARD VII *as he exits with* COURTIER. *She then looks to* MAYOR INGRAM *before dashing off.* MAYOR INGRAM *is left a alone.*

MAYOR INGRAM (*despairingly*). CHRIST!

Exit MAYOR INGRAM *through the centre-stage doors.*

The chaise longue and tray are removed.

Scene Seven

Enter the ENSEMBLE, *who sing a much darker version of 'Oh I Do Like to Be Beside the Seaside'. It's maddening.*

We are now outside Batwa's house.

Enter COLONEL HARRIS *through the centre doors with cases in hand. He hurries off into the yard.*

Enter BATWA *from the same doors. He carries with him a case. He locks the door, feeds the keys through the letter box, and goes to follow the colonel.*

Enter a broken JOANNA *from the yard.* BATWA *spots her.*

BATWA. Joanna?

JOANNA. –

BATWA (*gently*). Joanna??

JOANNA. 'Ow can I 'av got it all so wrong? – When I was the one who needed to be saved all along.

BATWA *goes to move closer to* JOANNA. JOANNA *steps back.*

BATWA. Joanna –

JOANNA. I just wanted to be *seen*, just for *one* day, because unless you're seen, you cannot be loved.

BATWA. Joanna, I'm leaving. I'm going home.

JOANNA (*disbelief*). No yer not.

BATWA. Yes I am.

JOANNA. No yer not, because if you leave, I ain't got no-else.

BATWA (*gently*). Joanna, I was always going back, my people need me.

JOANNA. *I* need you.

BATWA. I need to go home.

ACT TWO, SCENE SEVEN 111

JOANNA. But why?? You ain't been back in years, I doubt it'll even be the same.

BATWA. I agree. But you remind me, that try though I may, I can't outrun from who I really am: a chief who is also a *coward*; a chief who, in his people's time of need, got scared and ran away to the circus.

You couldn't begin to imagine some of the things I've seen. I doubt anyone I love will be alive when I get back. But that's why I didn't want you to meet the King. Because where I come from, a crown isn't a good thing. It stands for power; the unjustifiable imbalance of, entitlement, bloodshed, slavery, murder – and grief.

I might not be a king, Joanna, but like him I bear a responsibility, a *duty* to others. I forgot that, and so my duty has now turned into a debt, and one I wish to pay back.

So I am going, and I wish you the best of luck for tomorrow.

BATWA *exits through the yard.*

Enter MR BACON *from the other side of the yard. Neither* JOANNA *nor* BATWA *see him.*

JOANNA (*calling after him*). Wait! What if I told yer I ain't doing it no more? The pageant! Coz I ain't! It was stupid idea. You were right!

BATWA. That's your decision, Joanna, not mine.

JOANNA. So what, that's it then? Ain't nuffing I say gonna change yer mind? Mr Batwa?! Mr Batwa?! You're not coming back, are ya?

BATWA *turns to* JOANNA.

BATWA. A good performer knows when the curtain should fall.

Exit BATWA, *leaving a badly wounded* JOANNA.

MR BACON (*tenderly*). Joanna?

JOANNA *hears* MR BACON *but remains staring after* BATWA.

Joanna?

JOANNA. You can say what you like,
I ain't changing me mind.

MR BACON (*pleading*). Joanna *please*. I'm begging ya.

JOANNA. I said no.

JOANNA *goes to exit*.

MR BACON (*calling after her*). Then if you won't do it for me, would yer do it for the Kursaal? Because she's sick, Joanna.

JOANNA *is wounded again. She slowly looks towards* MR BACON.

It's true, Joanna. She's sick, she ain't well for a while nah. I bin doing me best to look after 'er, but she's bleeding aat: the accounts are dry, the money's gone. All of it. Just a simple case of overspend, nuffing more. But if she doesn't 'av money pumped into 'er – and soon – like the kinda money an international beauty pageant with a Senegalese princess could bring, she won't survive. And the shame that will bring to not only me, but my wife – who I love more than life itself – will be extraordinary, but nothing compared to the hurt and humiliation the people of this taan will feel if that building goes under and sits there rotting for years to come.

To the rest of the world, that's all it is – a building; nothing but bricks and mortar – but to Southenders – like us – it's family. Lose the Kursaal, and you will forever 'av a taan in mourning; because that's what grief is: love.

No princess, no money, no Kursaal, just scandal. And that's the last thing the town needs.

Beat.

Joanna? *Please*, I'm begging ya.

JOANNA. I said, no.

From the other side of the yard, enters MRS BACON *with* EVE, *a young Black/mixed-raced girl, aged seven.*

MRS BACON (*chirpily*). Hello, Princess Dinubolu!

ACT TWO, SCENE SEVEN   113

JOANNA *turns to see* MRS BACON *and* EVE *standing there.*

Princess, I'd like to introduce you to a little friend of mine. This is Eve. Say 'ello to Princess Dinubolu, Eve.

EVE. Hello.

MRS BACON (*patronisingly*). Eve, that's not what we practised, is it?

EVE *slowly makes her way over to* JOANNA. *She is in awe – she has never seen anyone so beautiful in all her life.* JOANNA *watches her.*

Eve 'erself was in a competition at the Kursaal a few years back, weren't you, Eve?

EVE. Yes.

Upon reaching JOANNA, EVE *stands and stares at her. A moment, as the two look at each other.*

MRS BACON (*getting her to hurry up*). Eve...

EVE *looks back at* MRS BACON, *before she returns her gaze to* JOANNA, *and curtsies.*

You know, Princess Dinubolu, when I told Eve she was going to be meeting a *real* princess, she was very excited – weren't you, Eve?

EVE. Yes.

MRS BACON. Couldn't believe 'er luck. And then when I told 'er she could come to the pageant tomorra daan at the Kursaal, well she was absolutely frilled, weren't you, Eve?

EVE. Yes.

MRS BACON. Coz we are going to be seeing you tomorra at the beauty pageant, aren't we Princess Dinubolu? – Aren't we?

JOANNA *looks at* EVE.

JOANNA. Yes.

MRS BACON. Good. Now say goodbye Eve.

EVE. Goodbye, Your Majesty.

> EVE *curtsies*.

MRS BACON (*gesturing to* EVE). Parsley.

> MR BACON *encourages* EVE *to go along with him*.

MR BACON (*gently*). Come on.

> *Exit* MR BACON *and* EVE. EVE *turns and looks at* JOANNA *as she leaves*.

MRS BACON (*sincerely*). Nah, you might not fink so, but we're all just tryna survive.

> *Exit* MRS BACON.

> JOANNA *is left alone. Like a soldier in battle, she is becoming tired, her wounds are now hurting her.*

JOANNA. This feeling feels, strangely familiar: fear. When all you want to do is run away and hide, you'll want to retreat – just like the estuary, but like it, you'll always have to come back sometime – and if I think about it, ain't turning just the tides way of talking?

And scared though I am, perhaps I owe it to the estuary – the one thing that has ever been constant in my life – to listen. And it's telling me, that perhaps this ain't about no pageant anymore – perhaps it hasn't been along, but a call to arms; a duty to serve a cause greater than myself and I find myself at this time, so far out at sea, that to swim against the current, back to the safety of the shore, feels impossible.

Estuary or sea, does it really matter? Princess or not, really, does it matter? When anyone can be a Queen, but a real Queen wears the crown, she doesn't let the crown wear her.

So, Kursaal – I'm coming for yer. Essex – I'm coming for yer. Empire – I'm coming for yer.

Now, LET'S GO GET THAT BLOODY TIARA!!

> JOANNA *punches the air before exiting through the yard*.

Scene Eight

It's now the day of the Miss Southend 1908 Beauty Pageant.

We are outside the Kursaal.

The BAND *begin to play an array of national anthems (USA, Germany, Belgium, Serbia, Norway, France, finally ending with 'Pomp and Circumstance' to represent Britian).*

As the band play, several things happen:

The double doors open to reveal BERNARD *and* REGINALD, *who roll out a red carpet and together begin to prepare the stage for the pageant: decorations are hung over the doors and pillars. Together they hoist a large banner that reads, 'Miss Southend Beauty Pageant 1908', etc.*

Onto the stage, from the yard, enters a rather out-of-breath MRS BUGLE, *who creeps backstage through the stage-right door.*

Through the centre-stage doors enter MAYOR INGRAM, *and* MR BACON, *who walk down the red carpet.*

As they do, through the yard and onto the stage enter the contestants: PEACHES, ELISE, SNEZANA, INGEBORG, FRIEDA *and* VIOLET (*who has* HARRIET *in tow*). VIOLET *stands away from and gawping at the competitors. The pageant girls all hug and greet one another with great enthusiasm – welcome to the sisterhood.*

MR BACON, *suddenly spotting a seemingly uninvited* HARRIET, *darts over to her, and grabs her by the arm.*

MR BACON. What are you doing 'ere? I told ya, yer not enterin'!

    HARRIET *looks at her arm and, realising what he's done,* MR BACON *immediately removes his hand.*

HARRIET. I know. I'm not. I'm just helping Violet, aren't I, Violet?

VIOLET (*turning to* MR BACON). She's with me.

    VIOLET *puts her hand out for* HARRIET *to take. She does so.* ELISE *spots* VIOLET *and so walks over to her.*

ELISE (*friendly*). You are Violet??

VIOLET. I am, yes.

ELISE. I like it, your name, and the colour.

VIOLET. Thank you.

ELISE. I am Elise. This is Peaches – (PEACHES *waves*.) Snezana – (SNEZANA *waves*.) Ingeborg – (INGEBORG *waves*.) and Frieda – (FRIEDA *waves*.)

ALL THE GIRLS. Hi!!!

ELISE. We are waiting for one girl, yes? The princess, she is not here yet, no?

    Enter an overly confident PRINCESS DINUBOLU *from the yard, being followed by* MR SOUTHEND STANDARD. *As she dictates to him, he takes notes.*

PRINCESS DINUBOLU. People have told me that only cream-and-pink little English misses can win and that your judges have no eye for any other sort. I wish to prove them wrong, and show England is fair to all-comers, even if they are chocolate-coloured.

    For you see my regime is very different to this of English girls. Every morning, I bury myself up to my neck in sand. Why? Because nothing makes the skin so velvety.

MR BACON (*through gritted teeth*). Good morning, Princess Dinubolu.

PRINCESS DINUBOLU (*arrogantly*). It's 'Mr Bacon', isn't it? I must insist you greet me accordingly.

    PRINCESS DINUBOLU *holds out her right hand for him to kiss; he reluctantly does so.*

    Beat as everyone looks to one another.

MR BACON (*affronted*). Right, come on then girls! (*Gesturing upstage*.) This way!

MR BACON *gestures for* PRINCESS DINUBOLU *and* MR SOUTHEND STANDARD *to walk along the red carpet – they do, and exit. All the others girls then follow on behind.*

BERNARD *and* REGINALD *roll up the red carpet as the girls go. Together the* COUNCILLORS *close the centre-stage doors.*

MAYOR INGRAM *gestures for* MR BACON *to quickly go and get the tiara.*

MR BACON *returns holding a small red cushion on which rests a diamond tiara.*

Scene Nine

We are on the main stage inside the Kursaal.

The BAND *play music. It's big and bold, and eventually morphs into a vamp that plays underneath* MAYOR INGRAM*'s introduction.*

MAYOR INGRAM (*addressing the audience*). Ladies and Gentlemen, one and all, bonjour, willkommen, ciao, ni hao, and good evening to each and every one of you here, tonight, at the world-famous Kursaal!!

I'm Mayor Ingram, and on behalf of myself, my fellow councillors – (*Gesturing to* MR BACON.) Mr Bacon – manager of the Kursaal – and the good people of Southend-on-Sea, I would like offer you our humbled and most heartfelt thanks, for attending what can only be described as the event of the year, the *Miss Southend 1908 Beauty Pageant*!!

The audience cheer.

Ladies and gentlemen, without further ado, allow me to present to you – THE GIRLS!!

Suddenly all the doors fly open to reveal PEACHES, VIOLET, ELISE, SNEZANA, INGEBORG, PRINCESS DINUBOLU *and* FRIEDA *all standing there in their pageant-attire glory. In cannon, the contestants step out from the doors.*

A dance sequence ensues. It's fun, camp, full of energy! There are sequences, formations, it's Edwardian meets sexy; the odd roll of a shoulder, the occasional flash of ankle.

During the dance, the girls approach the audience to proudly announce where they are from:

SNEZANA. Serbia!

ELISE. Belgium!

FRIEDA. Germany!

PEACHES. The United States of America!

VIOLET. Ingerland!

PRINCESS DINUBOLU. Senegal!

INGEBORG. Norway!

At one point in the dance, VIOLET *trips and* ELISE *helps her.*

Once the dance has ended the PAGEANT GIRLS *all pose.*

MAYOR INGRAM (*somewhat condescending*). Bravo, girls, but oh dear, I'm afraid it's time to say 'au revoir' to several of our contestants – and so, without further ado – and in no particular order – it's goodnight to you, Miss Serbia –

SNEZANA *steps back.*

and so long farewell, better luck next time, to you, Miss Norway –

INGEBORG *steps back.*

SNEZANA *and* INGEBORG *exit.*

ACT TWO, SCENE NINE   119

And so now we move on our second round –

All of a sudden we hear a bugle being played. It's coming from backstage. It sounds like a call-to-arms.

Suddenly, from stage-right, enters HARRIET, *who is wearing a long coat. She makes her way to downstage-centre, sounds her bugle once again and announces to the audience –*

HARRIET. HURRAH FOR THE WOMEN'S SOCIAL AND POLITICAL UNION!! WOMEN, REMEMBER YOUR DIGNITY!!

HARRIET *then unbuttons her coat, turns around to face upstage and flashes those around her.*

The reaction of those onstage (Including the BAND.*) is one of complete and utter horror.* HARRIET *then turns around to face the audience and to reveal that she has on an apron, across which she has painted the words* '*VOTES FOR WOMEN!*'

VOTES FROM WOMEN!! DEEDS NOT WORDS! DEEDS NOT WORDS!!

She looks to VIOLET.

VIOLET. DEEDS NOT WORDS!

HARRIET *and* VIOLET (*nodding*). DEEDS NOT WORDS!!

They continue chanting.

Enter BERNARD *and* REGINALD. *They* (*along with everyone except* VIOLET *and* PRINCESS DINUBOLU) *try their best to restrain* HARRIET. HARRIET *fights back.*

In the process of restraining HARRIET, ELISE, FRIEDA *and* MAYOR INGRAM *are all punched in the face – their noses begin to bleed, clothes are torn.* ELISE *and* FRIEDA*'s once-immaculate hairstyles are now completely wrecked. There is also a moment where in a panic,* MR BACON *hands to Joanna the tiara, on its cushion.* JOANNA *takes it and stares at it.*

REGINALD *and* BERNARD *drag* HARRIET *off.*

HARRIET *sings as she exits…*

Song – 'Rise Up Women!' to the tune of 'John Brown's Body'

HARRIET.
**Rise up, women, for the fight is hard and long
Rise in thousands signing loud a battle song
Right is might, and in its strength we shall be strong
And the cause goes marching on –
Glory, Glory, hallelujah! Glory, Glory, hallelujah!
Glory, Glory, hallelujah! The cause goes marching on!**

ELISE, FRIEDA, PRINCESS DINUBOLU, PEACHES *and* VIOLET *all slowly go back to their places and pose.*

A slightly out breath (and very aware of his dishevelled appearance) MAYOR INGRAM *steps forward.*

MAYOR INGRAM *(trying to remain professional).* My sincerest apologies for the interruption, ladies and gentlemen. I think it would be fair to say that we can now say adieu to you, Miss Belgium, and adios, ta-ta for now to you, Miss Germany.

ELISE *and* FRIEDA *exit, limping and wiping the blood from their noses.*

(Still trying to retain control.) We shall now be taking a short break, but we'll be back in five.

The BAND *plays exit music.*

VIOLET *marches over to* MAYOR INGRAM *and gestures to him that she wants a word. They argue as they exit. Exit also* MR BACON, *along with* PEACHES, VIOLET *and* PRINCESS DINUBOLU.

Enter MRS BUGLE *onto the balcony from stage-right. She anxiously waits.*

Enter PRINCESS DINUBOLU *onto Juliet's balcony. She perches, looking over the edge.*

ACT TWO, SCENE NINE 121

MRS BUGLE (*gently*). Joanna…

JOANNA *looks anxiously towards* MRS BUGLE.

Joanna. I assure you, you needn't worry. I've no intention of telling a soul, I promise.

JOANNA. Then why are you here?

MRS BUGLE. Because I wanted to say that I'm sorry, and that you can come home now.

JOANNA *is wounded. This time it's a different kind of pain; it's a release.*

JOANNA. I've missed you.

MRS BUGLE (*sincerely*). I've missed you too, so come home, please.

JOANNA. I can't.

MRS BUGLE. Why?

JOANNA. Because though I miss you, I don't miss the way you make me feel – and really I fink part of you just wants me to come 'ome so you can feel betta.

MRS BUGLE. That's not true.

JOANNA (*sad*). It is, it's just you can't see it yet – (*Disappointed.*) and that's okay.

MRS BUGLE. But home is where you belong.

JOANNA. Wrong. I belong only to myself.

Enter MR BACON. *He spots* MRS BUGLE *and addresses her.*

MR BACON (*reprimanding*). What you doing up 'ere? You're not allowed backstage.

MRS BUGLE. I know but –

MR BACON. Then may I kindly ask you to go back to your seat or I'll 'av yer escorted off the premises.

MRS BUGLE *looks at* JOANNA.

MRS BUGLE (*sincerely*). Good luck, Your Majesty. It's been a pleasure.

MRS BUGLE *exits*. MR BACON *looks to* JOANNA.

MR BACON (*chirpily*). Nearly there. Off yer pop! I'll be daan in a sec.

JOANNA *stares at* MR BACON.

What is it? What you finking?

JOANNA. Nuffin.

MR BACON (*encouragingly*). Well go on then! I'll be daan in a sec.

Exit JOANNA. *Enter a rather out-of-breath* BERNARD.

BERNARD. Mr Bacon, sir – Mayor Ingram says there's been a slight change of plan.

MR BACON (*concerned*). What 'change of plan'?

BERNARD. He says his daughter's demanded there be a slight change to procedure. He says he'll tell you more when he sees you –

Music begins.

– which is probably now as it's about to start.

MR BACON *leaves in a great hurry. Exit* BERNARD.

Enter VIOLET, PEACHES, PRINCESS DINUBOLU *and* MAYOR INGRAM *to the stage*.

They are followed by MR BACON, *who holds the small red cushion on which rests the tiara*.

MAYOR INGRAM. And so here we are, the moment you've all been waiting for, the moment of truth, the moment when one, and only one, of our three finalists: Miss Peaches Dubois of the United States –

PEACHES *waves*.

– Miss Violet May Ingram of England –

VIOLET *waves*.

– or Her Royal Highness, Princess Dinubolu of Senegal

PRINCESS DINUBOLU *doesn't wave*.

– shall be crowned queen.

VIOLET *clears her throat*.

MAYOR INGRAM *looks to* VIOLET.

And a twist.

(*Turning back to address the audience*.) No longer shall *I* be deciding the winner, but you, our audience.

And how shall this be done – (*Looking to* VIOLET.) *fairly*?

Well, Mr Bacon here shall place his hand over each of the contestants. An official with a stopwatch –

Enter REGINALD *with a timer around his neck, plus a clipboard and pencil*.

– shall record the length of the applause, while another –

Enter BERNARD.

– with his hand to his ear, shall estimate the volume of the cheers.

So, LET THE JUDGING COMMENCE!

Mr Bacon.

MAYOR INGRAM *encourages a confused* MR BACON *to make his way to the centre* – MR BACON *does so*.

We now invite you, our audience, to applaud for who you would like to see be crowned your *Queen of Southend*. Loudest cheer wins.

Let us begin with, Contestant Number One!!

PEACHES *makes her way over to* MR BACON. MR BACON *hovers the crown over* PEACHES.

Prediction: The cheers will be rather minimal, and so MAYOR INGRAM *pulls a rather patronising sad face*.

Contestant Number Two!!

VIOLET *makes her way over to* MR BACON. MR BACON *lifts the crown above* VIOLET*'s head.*

Prediction: The cheers will be minimal again or a bit louder than PEACHES, *and so a grimacing* MAYOR INGRAM *gestures to* MR BACON *to move on to the last contestant.*

Allow us to present, Her Royal Highness, Contestant Number Three!

PRINCESS DINUBOLU *makes her way over to* MR BACON. MR BACON *lifts the crown over* PRINCESS DINUBOLU*'s head.*

The crowd will go wild!!

A concerned MAYOR INGRAM *looks to* MR BACON. *He gestures for* BERNARD, REGINALD *and* MR BACON *to join him – they do so. An intense discussion follows.*

Ladies and gentlemen, one and all. Please be upstanding for *your* Miss Southend 1908...

Suddenly confetti is fired into the yard, the BAND *play music that is dark, strange, mystical. From upstage doors emerge any actors who are not onstage at this time.*

The ENSEMBLE *– no longer their characters – change to a state of neutral, they are unapologetically themselves.*

All slowly exit upstage through the doors – all except PRINCESS DINUBOLU/JOANNA.

She watches the crown move out of her reach.

A moment of silence as JOANNA *turns to face the audience.*

JOANNA (*addressing the audience*). This is it, isn't it?

This is the moment.

The moment of the words – of all, and any of the words we like.

And an *overwhelming* sense for me to share with you something new, something meaningful – something true.

And so what do you say when you have only one chance to speak, one chance to address the entire globe?

Because, I should. Who knows, maybe I am? – Right now.

Perhaps I already have?

But were you ready to listen? Are you ready to listen?

JOANNA *closes her eyes and listens.*

Silence.

A world of noise and silence, dancing together. How can we have all the words and all the silence, all at the same time?

A truth.

There isn't anything that I could tell you here, now – that deep down, you don't know already.

But to find it, to find that truth, your truth, it will mean you having to sit in your own silence. And you probably won't like it, but you owe it to yourself to be brave.

I won't say that what you find isn't your fault, who am I to say that, I don't know, and I don't know you, but right now, I *see* you, beautiful, beautiful you.

When was the last time you met you?

Scene Ten

All of a sudden, through the centre-stage doors creeps in EVE *holding the tiara behind her back. She walks over to* JOANNA, *curtsies, and hands it to her. A disappointed* JOANNA *does not take it.*

JOANNA. I didn't win.

   EVE *smiles.*

EVE. Oh yes you did.

JOANNA. No, really, I didn't.

Beat.

EVE. Is that what you think matters? You matter to *me*.

JOANNA takes the tiara and places it on EVE's head.

JOANNA (*with a smile*). I like your name, Eve.

EVE. That's right.

JOANNA begins to cry. She's exhausted.

JOANNA. I'm so tired, Eve.

EVE takes JOANNA by the hand.

EVE. I know – you rest – (*Looking out to the audience.*) I'll take over.

EVE leads JOANNA off through the centre-stage doors. The doors close.

The End.

And then a jig.

SHAKESPEARE'S GLOBE

Shakespeare's Globe is a world-renowned theatre, education centre, and cultural landmark.

Inspired and informed by the unique historic playing conditions of two beautiful, iconic theatres, our diverse programme of work harnesses the power of performance, cultivates intellectual curiosity, and excites learning to make Shakespeare accessible for all.

'I'll call for pen and ink, and write my mind'
William Shakespeare (*Henry VI Part 1*)

The Globe has been a proud producer of new plays since 1599.

In recent times in our wooden 'O', Shakespeare has sat side by side with some of our most established and celebrated contemporary playwrights and poets, alongside writers taking their first steps in the craft of playwriting.

> 'This is a landmark moment in the history of Shakespeare's Globe'
> *The Independent* on *Emilia*

Under the Artistic Directorship of Michelle Terry, the Globe has produced and presented new plays, adaptations, translations and interventions by:

Abi Zakarian, Aisha Zia, Amanda Wilkin, Amy Ng, Amy Trigg, Ben Hales, Catherine Mayer, Charlie Josephine, Chinonyerem Odimba, Chloë Moss, Ella Hickson, Eloise Pennycott, Emma Frankland, Es Grange, Eve Leigh, Gilbert Kyem Jnr, Hanan al-Shaykh, Hannah Khalil, Hanan al-Shaykh, James McDermott, Jasmine Naziha Jones, Jeanette Winterson, Jenifer Toksvig, Jenet Le Lacheur, Joe Hill-Gibbins, Kat Rose Martin, Katie Hims, Kelly Burke, Kelly Jones, Kerry Frampton, Laura Lomas, Lily Bevan, Lisa Hammond, Lucy Sheen, Matilda Feyiṣayọ Ibini, Matt Hartley, Morgan Lloyd Malcolm, Nicola Werenowska, Nicôle Lecky, Olivia Wakeford, Philip Ishak Arditti, Philippa Gregory, Rachael Spence, Ric Renton, Rory Mullarkey, Sabrina Mahfouz, Sami Ibrahim, Sandi Toksvig, Sara Shaarawi, Shamser Sinha, Simon Armitage, Stella Duffy, Suhayla El-Bushra, Tabby Lamb, Tanika Gupta, Tassa Deparis, Timberlake Wertenbaker, Tom Stuart, Travis Alabanza and Winsome Pinnock.